Stephen Wyatt

Antidote to the Crisis of

Stephen Wyatt

Antidote to the Crisis of Leadership

Opportunity in Complexity

DE GRUYTER

ISBN 978-3-11-079592-9
e-ISBN (PDF) 978-3-11-079629-2
e-ISBN (EPUB) 978-3-11-079636-0

Library of Congress Control Number: 2023952203

Bibliographic information published by the Deutsche Nationalbibliothek
The Deutsche Nationalbibliothek lists this publication in the Deutsche
Nationalbibliografie; detailed bibliographic data are available on the internet at
http://dnb.dnb.de.
© 2024 Walter de Gruyter GmbH, Berlin/Boston

Cover image: Hybert Design
Typesetting: York Publishing Solutions Pvt. Ltd.
Printing and binding: CPI books GmbH, Leck

www.degruyter.com

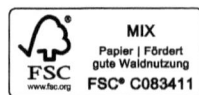

FSC
www.fsc.org
MIX
Papier | Fördert
gute Waldnutzung
FSC® C083411

Advance Praise for
Antidote to the Crisis of Leadership

Insightful and thought provoking, *Antidote* is a treasury of concepts and illustrative examples by a management veteran with a proven track record of business growth, financial impact and people development. A truly actionable reading for leaders who have the desire to make something happen in a world of complexity and instabilities.

Alessandro Bogliolo, former CEO, Tiffany & Co.

I've known Steve in various professional capacities during a span of almost 25 years. What's remarkable is his consistent focus on supporting others to be the best they can be whilst successfully navigating turbulence and complexity. In this book, Professor Wyatt shares insights and advice as well as a strong nudge that we should all be striving to make tomorrow better for everyone. His writing style is easily accessible, the book is enriched with comments from leaders globally, representing a wide variety of entities; private and public, government and commercial, charity, public service, education and military. A fascinating and thought-provoking message.

John Vamvakitis, Managing Director, Google for Education

Steve's work always provokes new insights and deep reflections, and *Antidote* is no different. I am always amazed by his ability to explain a complex issue like the evolving role of leadership in present times, in a simple and pragmatic way. In these times when that pause every leader needs is elusive, this book is a must read to connect with who you are and how you can expand and sustain your impact.

Atul Khosla, Founder, Leadership et` Humanite` LLC, Chicago, USA

We are facing a number of global crises, particularly in the areas of environment, health, economic inequality and geo-political stability. Navigating these crises responsibly, responding to challenges with awareness of the implications across geographies, communities and timeframes, and making decisions that will contribute to shaping a better future for all requires a new level of leadership. Those who have the courage and ability to step forward to lead during these 'decisive years for humanity and the planet' will find a great deal of inspiration and wisdom in this book. Steve Wyatt has expertly curated and reflected on his own experiences and those of others to craft a guide for the leaders we need now. I highly recommend reading it.

Sarah Gillard, CEO of A Blueprint for Better Business

Steve has pointed out one of the key challenges of leaders today – the need to lead in uncertainty and complexity. He has deftly distilled from his own experience together with multiple perspectives from global leaders across different continents into four 'A's, an antidote for today's global leadership crisis. *Antidote* is a timely book full of evergreen insights for guiding leaders to lead in an uncertain future.

Chin-Siong Seah, President, Singapore Institute of Management

This book is quite remarkable, both profoundly insightful and practical. Substance to make you stop and think and guidance for how to apply the insights. Professor Wyatt has decades of work as a senior leader and working with others, board members and executives alike; what he has achieved with this book is to combine all those voices and perspectives into a set of insights for how to manage, how to lead in the complex and accelerated world of today. It is essential reading for anyone seeking to avoid mediocracy or succumb to failure as a leader. It is insight and reminder if you are already an established leader and essential guidance for those who are setting out on their career.

Professor David Lee, SUSS and NUS, Chairman, Global Fintech Institute

Antidote distills insights and couples them with the latest academic research to deliver a compelling perspective on the shifting needs of leadership. In addition to reframing the challenges of leadership in the coming decade, he also provides actionable strategies for both individuals and teams to structurally build relevant capabilities. I have already begun implementing these approaches into my leadership team's professional development.

Colin Marson, Director, Google for Education, Asia Pacific

Stephen makes a significant contribution in advancing our understanding of leadership by collecting perspectives across industries and from experts across various cultures. He goes further by putting these insights through a very intuitive and logical organizing set of principles embodied in the 4-A's, which define effective leadership practices positioned to increase the probability of success. *Antidote* makes a significant statement on how leaders can develop their personal capabilities and enhance those of the people they lead.

Dr. James R. Andrade, Head Catapult Executive
Leadership & Innovation Institute

Professor Wyatt has achieved something remarkable. This book is a combination of both profundity and pragmatism, rigour and simplicity, depth and breadth. This book reflects his decades of work with senior executives and organisations across the world, while also drawing on research, expert input from thought leaders, and personal leadership insight from CEOs. If you are looking for the antidote to mediocre performance, and even worse, complete obsolescence in an era of disruption, then this is the book to read. Wyatt's advice, if followed carefully, will surely help you fulfil your potential as a leader, and help you transform your organization, whatever your sector or profession.

Peter Lorange, Honorary President, IMD, Chairman of S. Ugelstad Invest.

The impacts of poor and outdated leadership are profound; the crisis of leadership extends throughout all organisations, and across every sector. The impacts of this transcend deeply, affecting productivity, retention, performance and ultimately value. In *Antidote*, Steve Wyatt has produced an exceptional aid to change the paradigm – a way to rethink and re-energise leadership in the fourth industrial revolution.

Kit Hawkins, Executive Director, Sustainability & Renewable Energy

Steve Wyatt recognises that while leading and leadership are immensely complex, good leadership can only be built on a foundation that is clear and straightforward. *Antidote* cuts through the noise and provides a simple framework built around four key principles, Aspire, Ally, Adapt, Accelerate, that emerge from his research, and that everyone wanting to improve their leadership practice should acknowledge and adopt to create better environments for their followers to succeed in.

Roddy Millar, Editorial Director, *Developing Leaders Quarterly*

Antidote
... to the crisis of leadership

1. Aspire
Stand firm on the Purpose, Values and Stakeholder Interests that you choose to represent. 'Aspire' is about having personal goals and values, while 'inspire' is about motivating and influencing others through actions, words, or achievements. If you don't aspire, how will you inspire others?

2. Ally
Connect and collaborate broadly whilst helping others to thrive. Alliances involve collaboration between independent entities for mutual benefit, while a hierarchy denotes an authority-based structure where one entity holds a position of higher power or control over another.

3. Adapt
Increase the Dynamic Capacity of the enterprise and the mobility of resources. 'Adaptable' emphasises the capacity to adjust and change as needed, even if the adjustments are substantial, while 'agile' places more emphasis on speed, flexibility, and the ability to navigate change through iterative processes.

4. Accelerate
Time is short, and your energies are finite; learn faster. 'Accelerate' emphasises increasing the pace of progress, while 'continuous' communicates the need for on-going, consistent development; both are important mindsets for leaders today.

"Whatever is true, whatever is noble, whatever is right, whatever is pure, whatever is lovely, whatever is admirable – if anything is excellent or praiseworthy – think about such things."
Philippians 4:8

Contents

Acknowledgements

Antidote would not have been possible without the inputs, comments, discussions, reviews, encouragement, and critiques by an extraordinary group of people. Thank you all. I would particularly like to thank those who have known me professionally and personally for two decades or more; I greatly appreciate both your challenge and support. I also want to thank individuals and the executive teams at each client organisation I support. Thank you for inviting me into your worlds, sharing your challenges and opportunities, concerns, and aspirations with me, and trusting me to help shape the journeys you are on.

To my family (Rachel, Hannah, Sophia, and Jonathan), thank you for tolerating the hours invested in research, writing, and editing. Thank you for your loving support and for encouraging me to reach out so broadly to ex-colleagues and contacts from previous chapters of my working life. Janet Bradshaw, thank you for reading through and pruning a very early draft; your tenacity deserves respect. Bernie Jaworski, thank you for providing the Foreword; you have provided invaluable insight and support in several of my initiatives over the years; I greatly appreciate your support and wisdom. Also, a big thank you to those who have read through the draft and provided positive and critical comments; your endorsement is humbling.

To everyone about to explore this book, I hope you find insights that enrich your thinking about how you lead, that you are motivated to put some into action, and that you share the 'antidote' with others.

Foreword

In today's rapidly changing world, there is a pressing crisis of leadership. The context in which leaders operate has shifted dramatically, requiring a new balance of skills and mindsets. Unfortunately, many individuals currently in leadership positions find themselves 'caught wrong-footed' by these changes, having learned how to lead in a now obsolete reality. Meanwhile, the expectations, visibility, and judgement placed on leaders have increased significantly, producing heightened stress and anxiety.

There is a shortage of leaders who can navigate the complexities of today's context. To have a better tomorrow, we need an antidote to this crisis in leadership. Professor Stephen Wyatt presents us with the antidote in this thought-provoking book. He acknowledges that traditional leadership and leadership development approaches are no longer adequate in the face of the 4th Industrial Revolution's dynamic and accelerated landscape. The key lies in equipping leaders with the four 'A's – Aspire, Ally, Adapt, and Accelerate – to create a positive impact and support sustainable development.

In my role as Chair at the Peter F. Drucker and Masatoshi Ito School of Management at Claremont Graduate University, I recognise the urgency and necessity of this call to action. We must enable a shift from individuals merely occupying leadership positions to instead becoming genuine leaders who are passionate about and capable of inspiring others towards a brighter future. Today's leaders must embrace complexity, uncertainty, and the need to swiftly adapt whilst acting to promote values and pursue a purpose that creates a better tomorrow.

I am sure you, like I, will enjoy reading the comments shared by the panel of leaders who contributed to this book. Each piece of advice reflects the unique journey and wisdom of its speaker, reinforcing the value of diverse perspectives and the notion that we can learn from one another. The collective wisdom presented here is a powerful resource for anyone seeking to become a better leader, whether emerging or already seasoned. By embracing the principles of the four 'A's and committing ourselves to the pursuit of impactful leadership, we can transform the crisis into an opportunity for positive change.

Professor Wyatt's work is a beacon of hope in a complex landscape. He challenges us to evolve our capabilities and be forces for good. The book empowers us to shape the future we desire and make a difference in the lives of others. I commend Professor Stephen Wyatt for this valuable contribution to the understanding and advancement of leadership. As we undertake our respective journeys as leaders, let us remember that the future is in our hands, and it is our responsibility to shape it for the better. I invite you to be a part of the antidote to the crisis of leadership and I wish you all the best in building the future you desire.

Bernard Jaworski, Peter F. Drucker Chair in Management
and the Liberal Arts, Claremont Graduate University

Preface

Writing this book was triggered when I was contacted by a partner of an executive search firm looking to fill a CEO position. What, I wondered, was the context that would prompt his outreach to me rather than scroll through LinkedIn looking at the ranks of executives currently in the same sector as his client? He responded that transformational leaders are in short supply, whereas the company already has sector knowledge.

Intrigued, I discussed this apparent scarcity of leaders with friends and colleagues from various sectors, countries and types of organisations; confirming the widespread concern for the shortage of leaders who are effective with today's context and challenges. Executives are being appointed into leadership roles for which they are not equipped. It's not good for them, leading to stress, anxiety, mistakes, and burnout. It's not good for the stakeholders, for the employees, for value creation or society more broadly.

It should not be surprising that there is a shortage of leaders with the capabilities required for today and tomorrow, as most executives have been observing, learning, and leading in yesterday's context. There are far fewer enterprises that have been 'born digital' than those that are being transformed by digital. Far fewer that empower talent from any generation, gender, or geography than those tweaking legacy culture and HR policies. Most leadership development activities focus on the 'tried and tested' competencies and practices, yet we need leaders to take us into the unfolding, uncertain future.

I set out to answer two questions: (1) What skills are needed to be successful as a leader today and tomorrow that are different from those required previously? (2) How can people develop these differentiating skills and mindsets? Over 50 leaders representing a wide variety of backgrounds and enterprises generously participated in structured interviews exploring these two questions. The format of this book emerged through these discussions as each contributor wanted to share their insights and provide encouragement to you. I have intertwined but kept the individual voices whilst also providing structure to the themes.

The antidote to the shortage of leaders equipped for the challenges of today and tomorrow is to broadly disseminate the knowledge of what skills are required and encourage individuals to enhance their repertoire; such is the purpose of this book. I do not critique the existing body of research and writing on leadership but focus on the skills that differentiate performance today. Evergreens of leadership such as Integrity, Vision and Judgement are not challenged nor diminished; I focus on the skills and mindsets that enable their effective practice.

The book describes four sets of attributes that equip leaders to thrive in this context. (1) Aspire: They aspire to make a positive impact; for the stakeholders they choose to represent, pursuing a purpose they are passionate about and standing firmly for the values they believe they should embody. (2) Ally: Leaders today succeed by forming relationships with others within and beyond their immediate organisations. There is a strong sense of mutual respect and trust, a commitment to helping each other individually and collectively to thrive. (3) Adapt: Today's context is highly dynamic, fast-changing, and uncertain. Leaders must be able to navigate their enterprises through turbulence, flexing the organisation and flowing the resources to the priority issues. (4) Accelerate: The breadth of issues, the speed of change and the rate of knowledge creation are all accelerating. Leaders must optimise their rate of learning if they are to remain relevant and continue to achieve impact.

I hope that you find this book to be thought-provoking and that it helps you to strengthen your leadership muscles. Each chapter concludes with suggestions for actions that you can take to build your impact as a leader in these dynamic times.

(1) **Pause.** The book contains my thinking on key themes and references to relevant scholarly works and perspectives; however, you may find the quotes from leaders globally to be the most helpful for you. As you read through each section, I hope some words catch your attention and stick with you.

(2) **Reflect.** You are as unique in the way that you lead as you are unique as an individual. As such, you must consider which leadership and growth aspects resonate with you and how they extend, reinforce, or contradict your insights and experiences.

(3) **Experiment.** Like trying on a new jacket in a store's fitting room before buying and wearing it out in the street, new behaviours should be experimented with in more controlled settings, before being fully adopted. An experimenter's mindset leads to more growth as we try out more actions, learn, adapt, and build, rather than looking for that one big new thing we can do and expecting to be expert with it immediately.

You don't need lofty goals to be a leader; you must have the desire and courage to make something happen. There is a shortage of leaders: those willing and able to make a difference. We need leaders with the skills, mindsets, and courage to lead well in today's context with a desire to achieve a positive impact. I hope that you are one of those people. As you read this book, know that everyone quoted here cheers you on to be the best leader you can be.

Contributors: The Panel

A huge debt of thanks is due to each of the leaders who have contributed their insights and reflections to this book. While all in leadership positions today, they represent a broad set of backgrounds, sectors, and types of enterprise. They are of 12 ethnicities, multiple nationalities, different age groups and genders. While respecting the confidentiality of individuals, it may also be useful to you, the reader, to have some idea of the profile of the leader whose comment you may be impacted by. As such, each of the quotes I have included in the book is accompanied by initials. Here, I provide a key (Table 1) describing each person's profile. As you read through the book, you may build a view of the personality of some of the specific leaders by collecting their quotes. Alternatively, select some specific individuals from the characteristics provided in Table 1 and then trace their comments throughout the book. All the panellists have contributed to this book to support you to thrive as a leader in the complex, challenging context of the 4th industrial revolution. A big 'thank you' to all who contributed.

Table 1

Initials	Gender	Ethnicity	Organisation Type	Age Range	Seniority
AB	M	European	Multinational	50–60	CEO
AJ	F	African-British	Elite Sports	30–40	Squad Leader
AW	M	African-British	Elite Sports	30–40	Team Leader
AI	M	British	Government Agency	40–50	CEO
AK	M	Indian	Multinational	50-60	Founder
BH	M	British	High School	30–40	Head
BJ	M	US	Thought-Leader	60+	Founder
WS	M	British	Environmental Services	50–60	Founder
BL	M	Chinese-Singapore	Multinational	50–60	President, Asia-Pacific

Initials	Gender	Ethnicity	Organisation Type	Age Range	Seniority
CE	F	White/Asian	Private Education	50–60	Chairman
CU	M	British	Consultant	40–50	Founder
CS	M	Chinese-Singapore	University	60+	President
CM	M	US	Multinational	40–50	Vice-President, Asia-Pacific
DH	M	Chinese	Multinational	40–50	Managing Partner (Asia)
DL	M	Chinese-Singapore	Investment Fund	60+	Founder
EB	F	European	NGO-Sustainability	40–50	Founder
EBW	F	British	Multinational	50-60	Director
HW	F	British	Religious Organization	60+	Local Head
IS	M	British	Multiple	60+	Chairman and Board Member
JA	M	African-American	Multinational	60+	VP, Asia
JV	M	US	Multinational	50-60	Global VP
JH	M	European	Multinational	40–50	Regional VP
KC	M	British-Indian	Consultant	40–50	Founder
KH	M	British	Environmental Services	40–50	Division Head
LB	M	British	Internet Start-Up	30–40	Founder
LR	F	European	Multinational	50-60	Director
SM	M	British	Coach and Consultant	40–50	CEO Charity

Initials	Gender	Ethnicity	Organisation Type	Age Range	Seniority
MG	M	White/Asian	Leadership Consultant	30–40	Leadership Team
MH1	F	US	Leadership Thought-Leader	60+	Founder
MH2	M	British	Business Consultant	40–50	Managing Partner
ML	M	European	Business Consultant	60+	Managing Partner
NH	M	British	Multinational	50–60	CEO
OL	M	British	Multinational	50-60	CEO
PC1	M	Irish	Multinational	40–50	C-Suite
PC2	M	British	Professional Association	50–60	CEO
PM	M	British	Multiple	60+	Board Director
PL	M	European	Multiple	60+	Board Director
RB	M	US	Leadership Coach	60+	Independent
RC	M	British	Multinational	50–60	Managing Director
RG	M	British	Incubator and Accelerator	50–60	Founder
RP	M	British	Multinational	50–60	Vice President
RS	M	US	University/ Business School	50–60	Academic
SB1	F	British	Multinational	40–50	Managing Director
SB2	M	Irish	Multinational	40–50	Managing Partner
SG	F	British	Non-Profit	50–60	CEO
SGJ	F	African-British	Elite Sports	30–40	Squad Leader

Initials	Gender	Ethnicity	Organisation Type	Age Range	Seniority
RW	F	Asian	Entrepreneur	50–60	President
SW	M	British	Portfolio	50–60	Chairman
TC	M	British	National Corporation	50–60	Director
TM	M	British	Elite Sports	40–50	CEO
TS	F	Caribbean	Government	40–50	Ambassador
WN	M	European	Business Consultant	50–60	Managing Partner

In addition to those cited in Table 1 and directly quoted in the book, I would like to thank the inputs from those who preferred not to be quoted directly. A special note of thanks to those leaders from military and religious organisations; your insight particularly helped steer my writing on values-based leadership and living with discipline.

PART ONE
Leadership Today

Chapter 1
Crisis, Complexity and Opportunity

The Function of Leadership Has Not Changed …

Leadership is influencing others. A definition of the function of leadership that I particularly like is 'to inspire and direct the energies of others in the achievement of goals, whilst promoting their emotional and physical wellbeing'. Without followers, there is no leader. There is a relationship and co-dependence between the leader and their followers, even if that follower is singular – just themselves. Leaders have an impact on other groups, such as customers, investors, suppliers, broader society, policy and lawmakers, governments, and nations. I align with the perspective that leadership is about exerting influence to undertake actions in pursuit of defined objectives. 'Leadership takes place in relationships, which are built through interactions with stakeholders – locally and globally, inside and outside the enterprise.'[1]

WS: What do I do as a leader all day? I don't 'do' anything. I manage, coordinate, and inspire staff – it's all about people, to get the best I can out of a disparate group of people. People are endlessly fascinating and different. So, a leader creates effective relationships with different staff, adjusting themselves to manage different people in different ways. Some need hands-off and some hands-on.

IS: The essence of leadership has not changed; a clearly articulated strategy rooted in customer needs with a clear economic model, communicate it well, work with a great team – but the context is accelerated and less stable, and followers' expectations have changed.

AJ: Identify a purpose and ignite passion and desire in others to unite them in a way that maximises the overall capacity to achieve lasting and meaningful impact for good.

CU: Be the change, changing before you have to – this is leadership.

Instability Is Not New

The 20th century witnessed some tumultuous changes and unexpected shocks; for example, the two world wars, the stock market crash (1929), the Spanish, Korean and Vietnam Wars. The unravelling of the British Empire. The switch to the US dollar as reserve currency. The energy crises and oil shocks of the 1970s. However, many (most notably in Western management and media) regarded the relative stability of the last decades of the 20th century and the beginning of the 21st century as setting a norm that would continue. It is worth noting that during this period of supposed stability, the Soviet Union collapsed, there was the Asian financial crisis, Japan suffered the debt crisis, and China started on a path of rapid economic growth (what it regards as a recovery to its previous level of global economic and political influence). A pandemic (SARS) caused lock-down across much of Asia. As the 21st century dawned, the promise of the internet was both inspiring and terrifying executives and investors, accompanied by a panicked rush to be 'Y2K ready'. In 2007–2008 we experienced the Global Financial Crisis, which was known as the 'American Financial Crisis' for those living in Asia at that time. The subsequent decade saw unprecedented floods of cash being released by central banks as stimuli (Quantitative Easing). The consequent bloated balance sheets and soaring valuations of many enterprises helped create over 1,000 'unicorn' companies (i.e., companies with a valuation of over US$1 billion without having yet produced consistent profits). This same period also saw the acceleration of the wealth gap in many societies and the increasing frequency and severity of disruptions caused by the climate. Russia, China, India, and others grew in confidence to display their dissatisfaction with and ultimately to weaken global institutions such as WTO, ICC, UN. More recently we have experienced the global Covid pandemic, war in Europe and the escalation of corporate and political scandals. Whether or not you think there ever was a period of technological, economic, and geopolitical stability, the future is not going to be stable. The world is in flux with the exponentially rising impact of technology, shifting geo-political landscape, loss of faith in public institutions, changing expectations for personal rights vs collective responsibility, the disintermediation of communication, and shifting sociodemographic order. In whichever sectors and countries we operate, the future (and the present) bears decreasing resemblance to the past.

BL: The world order tussle and geopolitical tensions amplify uncertainty in [a situation of] globalisation; Fear Of Missing Out (FOMO) increases the inclination for protectionism, hoarding, factions, and friend-or-foe considerations in trade pact decisions. These may tremendously impact leadership skills and capabilities – particularly those in global/regional leadership roles and where products need to be made in one or a few places and distributed to many nations.

AI: Leaders are conditioned by the environment. As a result of the pandemic and having to get through it, many leaders survived – therefore, they have a new positive outlook when facing challenges. It is not about resilience (hiding behind armour) but the capability to get through even the toughest conditions and challenges. A positive mindset is needed to get through the tough conditions. Now we have a talent shortage, supply-chain disruption, and high inflation – perhaps bigger challenges than Covid – but a sense that there is 'no mountain too high' – none that we can't climb and overcome.

CE: Over the next ten years, the balance of economic power will shift to China. Everyone should seek to understand how to engage with China – for mutual benefit – [and] also know the context in which decisions are made in China. All leaders need to have a China literacy to understand what is happening there as they increasingly grow economically, particularly the role they will take geopolitically and address issues globally, especially where the West doesn't engage.

The Demands on Leaders Have Changed

Increased visibility of systemic complexity. There is a greater awareness of the complexities of the contexts in which we lead. We must consider more factors, more unknowns and strive harder to become aware of the 'unknown, unknowns' (to paraphrase Donald Rumsfeld). However, there is an argument that complexity itself has not increased; the interdependencies, the systemic relationships and causes and effects were always there, but now the level of instability (speed of change and amplitude of volatility) has so increased that we must pay greater attention. Factors that were stable and had little importance for our decision-making now must be considered. Awareness of uncertainty is the new norm, accompanied by increased visibility of systemic complexity. The Covid pandemic caught most by surprise, some leaders (in government as in business) coped well and their enterprises emerged stronger, but many did not, they looked for sympathy, forgiveness, and hand-outs, they hoped to 'tough-it-out until everything returned to "normal"' and if their enterprises failed, they blamed extreme circumstances beyond their control. Now the expectation of stakeholders is that a competent leader will navigate successfully as uncertainty, volatility and complexity are ... certainties.

AK: Businesses are becoming increasingly complex (even those with strong tailwinds) – [there are] new challenges on instability in packaging, supply chain, staffing, etc. By contrast, board members and shareholders are demanding strong performance, as if the CEO can overcome all the challenges all the time; (this is historical thinking about a world that was more stable and predictable). It is a highly unpredictable environment, yet leaders are expected to find solutions. There are no clear answers or solutions.

SB1: You need to think enterprise-wide now – not to be parochial. What's best for the enterprise – not just your department? The challenges that we must respond to require an enterprise-wide mindset. Successful leadership should be doing this on a day-to-day basis, not just when in crisis.

PC1: Ability to deal with uncertainty and paradox – the reality [is that] we need to open our minds more, listen more, and with humility – very open-mindedly; understand where your own biases lie. We are in the true VUCA [volatility, uncertainty, complexity, and ambiguity] world, with many forces coming at us. We may be leaders, but we are still learning. We need a growth mindset.

CE: The pace of change is likely to accelerate further – driven by the development of technology. The rate of adoption is accelerating (we saw this in the pandemic).

A shortage of talent, people with the needed skills and depth of experience. The World Economic Forum expects that 44% of workers' skills will be disrupted in the five years from 2023 to 2027[2], related to a 23% churn of the labour market as many traditional jobs are displaced by technology and others using technologies are created. In this context, many individuals will be anxious about their jobs and the future relevance of their skill sets. It is estimated that six in ten workers (in OECD countries) will require retraining before 2027 (approx. 400 million people). The required pace and scale of upskilling and reskilling are unprecedented; the current capacity of adequate training is only half of that required. There will be a significant increase in competition between firms for suitably skilled individuals; the talent shortage will increase.

WS: The relationship between employee and employer has also shifted – there is a real shortage of labour – and, therefore, a shift in power in the relationship. What you can ask of an employee is limited – they can just leave and work elsewhere.

PC: People will go where the better, more adaptable leaders are. The companies where they are will thrive. It's the end of mediocre leadership – i.e., those with only the old style; I can't wait. I'm sick of mediocre leaders who are just political animals or, at best, have some technical skills they rely on.

Followers (employees) have greater expectations of their leaders, observe them with greater scrutiny and are more vocal in judging. The pervasiveness of social and other digital media has enabled a dramatic rise in the expectation for and visibility of leaders and other influencers. Individuals become followers if they 'like' what they see. Leaders increase in standing and influence as their follower base expands. Followers (whether employees, voters or otherwise) expect to see what the leader/influencer is doing and hear what they think on a wide range of issues, even those on which the leader/influencer has no informed insight!

PC: People are looking at you as an individual. What are the values you stand for? Are you human like us? Your humanity is much more evident than you think. What makes you tick? There is greater transparency now – and we expect more from our leaders.

AK: People expect more from their leaders – all the time. Personal recognition and support, not just designating resources or rewards. For instance, in China during the lockdown, some firms went out of their way to provide food supplies to their employees at home – but then the employees complained that they did not get a personal call from the country manager to check they were OK.

However, the expectation of communicating opinions on all topics, places undue pressure on leaders and increases the risk that they are caught out making factually incorrect or ill-informed statements.

RS: The challenge is that we are walking on eggshells – afraid to upset someone or some group every day. Leaders are criticised for what they do and what they don't do. In the US, this has put corporate communications teams into overdrive with statements about everything that happens in society. I was criticised for not having timely communication from the organisation to condemn a shooting event – of course, we condemn these things, but why should we be issuing statements several times a month about new developments we only know about from the news and on topics where we don't have expert informed opinion? Is the news we have heard accurate or complete or balanced? - we don't know - but we are chastised if we don't put out a comment on what the media has reported.

TM: People expect you to have a view on things now – there is no possibility of not having an opinion – not having a view is not neutral. There is nowhere to hide. There are no secrets.

OL: I agree that the environment is getting harder; there are internal and external dimensions. The internal domain is important as you are always under scrutiny, and employees are more expectant. The external domain is increasingly important due to social media and contagion. [It is an] immensely demanding and complex context.

Societal and wellbeing concerns. In many countries there is a much greater awareness and concern for environmental, societal and wellbeing issues; a heightened social consciousness. The seventeen Sustainable Development Goals[3] of the United Nations (first declared in 2015) are 'calls to action' that have helped to raise awareness and expectation that leaders – whether in business, government or other – will respond. Whatever your perspective is on these issues, they are factors shaping the thoughts and motivations of many and, therefore, cannot be ignored.

CE: We've seen what doesn't work – where there is poor leadership and individual country/organisation action. Now we need to come together to solve the big challenges that humanity faces.

The Crisis of Leadership

Corporations, governments, and individuals that fail to acknowledge or navigate this multi-dimensional, dynamic context underperform. My previous study tracked the share-price performance of companies (from various sectors) over five years (pre-Covid). On average there was a 40%+ difference in value creation between those that leant forward into uncertainty compared to those who failed to do so. Too many amongst the existing cadre of leaders neither know how, nor have the ability, to adjust for the demands of the new context. Traditionally, leaders have grown learning and building on the existing 'rules of the game' in their chosen context often by slowly accumulating direct experience or following role models. There's a crisis because leaders must now adopt behaviours and mindsets for the new context and the demands and expectations placed upon them. But there are few successful role models to observe and few opportunities for people already in leadership positions to learn how to adjust their approach. Many enterprises find themselves with cadres of executives maintaining traditional models of organisation and management practices, hoping they will suffice for a while longer. Executives trying to respond to the context and pressures of today whist using traditional practices and mindsets are likely to produce unintended and unwanted outcomes. As one panellist noted 'no one sets out to be irresponsible' yet scandals and examples of poor leadership abound. A few, too few, thrive; they achieve exceptional value growth, provide good employee experiences and deliver positive societal impact.

- **A shortage of leaders today and leaders in development.** There are not enough leaders, now or in development.[4] The People Officers of approximately three-quarters of major corporations surveyed[5] state that they do not have the leadership bench depth that they need now and are struggling to find enough capable and willing candidates to develop. Linked to this, executive search firms report that many senior executives are withdrawing from the talent market. Instead, they are seeking to develop a portfolio of roles wherein they can have more freedom and they are better able to distance themselves from the intense pressure to perform that might have led them to compromise their values and ethics.

- **Without the skills and mindsets required today.** Many leaders do not have the skills and mindsets required for today. Traditional approaches to embracing and managing talent, making decisions, understandings of risk and communicating have diminished effectiveness. Most of today's senior leaders have been trained, gained experience, and advanced their careers in contexts before the 4th Industrial Revolution. Their role models were great leaders in another era; would the approaches of Jack Welch or Steve Jobs be as effective today? Many existing leaders need to refresh their thinking and practices to increase their impact.

- **Failures of leadership are visible in scandals (corporate, political and charity).** Most notable are the corporate scandals that led to the collapse of 'giants' – such as Enron or Theranos. There also plenty of examples of 'poor' leadership which have been discovered, successfully prosecuted, and led to heavy fines. For example, the multi-billion-dollar settlements by companies GSK, Pfizer, HSBC, Goldman Sachs, Uber, Mercedes-Benz, and others. More numerous still are the companies with corrosive workplace cultures and exploitative employment policies that teeter on the edge of legality. While these only occasionally result in headline-grabbing lawsuits, it undermines millions of workers' emotional and possibly physical wellbeing.

- **Inattention to sustainable development.** Many bemoan the lack of leaders committed to pursuing outcomes linked to the betterment of society more broadly or the planet. Individual leaders pursue the outcomes they have individually elected to prioritise, whether personal or shareholder profit, national economic growth, or stability, social and environmental good – or seizing the natural resources of a neighbouring country. Every leader has biases, beliefs, fears, and cultural perspectives. While there are stand-out examples of leaders, such as Paul Polman (ex-Unilever), who successfully pursue sustainability goals alongside economic objectives, definitive role models remain few.

Implications for Leaders

Collaboration Not Command

Employees (or followers) stakeholders have significantly grown in power and influence. The result of a combination of factors: a shortage of talent with the required skills, greater mobility, increased scrutiny, and judgement of leaders, rising importance overall employee experience (purpose, flexibility, well-being, skills development, etc.). An approach of 'connect and collaborate' is required rather than 'command and control'. The leader must foster personal connectivity with the followers and appreciate that they are choosing to provide their support at the present time.

SGJ: Things have shifted in what people expect from the leader. I have to work harder in the individual relationships, make sure that [I hear] the bigger voices in the followers [and] ensure that they are on board with me, that we have alignment.

RC: Making the team more than transactional – stand for things together, emotionally invested in it together (e.g., a private, group goal, not just the corporate goal).

SB: See colleagues as everyone doing different roles – do not fixate on the hierarchy. Everyone is a human, and everyone has family and life issues, leader or not.

More Personal

Individuals want to know the personality of the leader, the values they hold, the mission they are pursuing and what that may mean for the would-be follower; employee, or voter. 'Does this leader care about me, my wellbeing, the stresses and strains in my life, my job security, the future relevancy of my skills?'

SG: Pre- vs post-Covid changes – leaders need to value the followers; approachability is critical for leaders. People want to feel more connected to the leader and the cause than before. Levels of compassion and empathy are already increasing and will continue to do so. People are more conscious now. How well am I and my wellbeing being looked after? What are we doing for the world and society?

AJ: Winning is not enough: People want more than this now. People used to accept negative behaviours whilst pursuing the goal of winning. [Now] they want to feel valued, appreciated, respected, nurtured – just as people, rather than athletes.

Leaders Under Increased Stress and Scrutiny

In this more complex and dynamic context, leaders must make more decisions quickly with less data and less certainty. Yet, followers have greater expectations of the leaders and have greater visibility. Data, as has always been, is not available on the future at the time when leaders must make decisions but in the context of today the future is less likely to be an extension of the past. A good process will not always result in good outcomes. Yet stakeholders, unhappy with the outcomes achieved have the benefit of hindsight when they examine the decisions made. The leader cannot be equally accountable to everyone on everything all the time. Yet the voice of a small, disaffected minority can be rapidly amplified millions of times by the simple clicking of 'like' or posting and reposting comments. Unsurprisingly, many senior experienced leaders are choosing to step away from prominent roles.

TM: Now – compared with ten years ago – things have changed significantly; the vulnerability and humanity of leaders. There is a need to hold a broader sense of accountability/responsibility. Deliver against the profit goals, 'yes', but there are other concerns – the profit goal is just one of the goals. For instance, European investors insist on seeing the ESG [Environmental, Social and Governance] goals hit, whereas our US investors insist on DEI [Diversity, Equity, and Inclusion].

AK: You have to remember that leaders are dealing with their own difficulties, pressures, and anxieties, as well as disruptions to themselves and those they care about. So, they have to deal with these disruptions as well as lead the organisations and teams. We are all human beings, and we all have our own challenges.

WS: What is new in leadership? It is easy to believe it (leadership) is getting harder. Generational shift, being purpose-led, an epidemic of mental stress, work-life boundary management. Leaders must lead while [they are] continuously facing new, unseen challenges.

In this environment, leaders must invest in their own resilience and wellbeing. The enterprise's performance and the ability to lead others appropriately depends on the leader being balanced and functioning well.

MH: There is always time for your family – for your interests, for your team. It's an investment. You invest in your team; you invest in your family, in exercise. It allows you to build better rather than slipping backwards. You must invest in your family and physical and mental health; your team and organisation will benefit.

OL: Caring is hard and can be debilitating. We can become too depleted. First, know yourself – when you are becoming too depleted, [such as] the quality of sleep, having a glass of wine earlier in the day than usual. Know the signs and react. Also, have others around you who can call you on it. They require you to always perform at your best – so they need permission to tell you that you are not at your best.

BJ: Leaders now explicitly invest in their mental health – mindfulness, spirituality, etc. How do you take care of yourself? What does that look like for you? Leaders need to take care of themselves – everyone is different, and every solution is unique for the individual.

Upskilling and Reskilling

As discussed above, a tremendous displacement is ongoing in the market for skills, with 6 in 10 workers needing to be reskilled over the next five years; the same is true for leaders. Leaders, whether seasoned or emergent, need to take ownership of their ongoing learning and development; creating their own experiences and communities of support to stay current, to adopt and hone the mindsets, techniques and approaches required for success in the context of the 4th Industrial Revolution.

Successful Leadership Today: Panellist Views

Below I have included quite a lot of quotes from the panel; you will see there are almost as many definitions of success as there are leaders quoted! As you read through them critically question what is being said and use the insights you extract to add to your understanding of leadership in the context of today.

SM: Success is making an impact at the level of society – anything short of that is dangerous – as now we see how everything is so interlinked. It's always been there, but it's more important than ever ... The formula that got us here is not working any more. We must find another way of being.

WN: [CEOs] need to have these three things ... (1) Knowing where you come from and who you are, (2) Your vision for the future – that people buy into, (3) Knowing how you as an individual will be able to lead the organisation in that direction.

MG: Success [is the] ability to bring together a high-performing team – my definition is 'leader-ship – it's about the 'ship' and not the leader'.

ML: A definition of success: Ensure that people follow you through inspiration, not power – through living certain values, which are more centred on improving society, etc.

PC2: Successful followership is the definition of successful leadership.

PM: Definition of successful leadership: 'unlock talent' – one person is not big enough – unlock the talent of the team through the leader ... The leader is talented in leadership; the others are experts in their domains.

IS: Get the results; define the metrics and get the measures and get results on those. Get everyone aligned [on the fact] that those are the metrics that matter.

SB: Success; achieving the right outcomes with minimum collateral damage. It used to be about outcomes irrespective of the 'cost' to the organisation, even if it lost trust and damaged its reputation.

AK: [It's about] having a sustained impact on yourself, the people around you, and the business. It is NOT time-dependent: not constrained by the next quarter, this year, the five-year strategy plan, your next promotion, etc. People want to believe in you for the long haul, not just for this period or project.

The Opportunity

In this dynamic, uncertain, and complex context, with a shortage of leaders, anyone can choose to try to lead, seeking to achieve the impact they are passionate about. Similarly, anyone can choose not to lead; to not stand up. The opportunity is here, now, if you want – to increase your impact; to be a part of the solution to crisis of leadership. You'll need the skills and mindsets discussed in this book –and courage too. You might be in a leadership position now or you might currently be focused on your development, in either case, I encourage you to refresh and update your thinking and approach. In this book, you will find a colourful 'palette' of different insights, examples, and personal reflections by successful leaders in today's world – but it is you who must paint your own picture. Time is short; identify steps you can take today.

Pause, Reflect and Experiment: Crisis, Complexity and Opportunity

(1) What's your personal view?
  - Has the context, function or demands on leaders changed?

(2) Is there a 'crisis of leadership' – do you feel or see it?
  - Who are the leaders of today that you admire?
  - What is it that they are doing that impresses you?
  - Are there enough great leaders today who are making a positive impact, helping to shape a better tomorrow?

---

(3) Do you explicitly explore, discuss and address uncertainty and systemic complexity?
  - Within the leadership team and with stakeholders.
  - Are you 'leaning in' and navigating effectively.

(4) Is there an opportunity for you to increase your impact as a leader for today and tomorrow?

The goal of this book is to support you to increase your effectiveness as a leader, which requires that you do things differently. Two simple techniques that can help transition from reading and thinking to doing are keeping a logbook of your thoughts and actions and sharing your journey with a colleague or friend.

(1) Logbook: Keeping a logbook is not very revolutionary, but it is effective. Whether a physical logbook or virtual, writing down your thoughts is powerful. Writing is slower and more deliberate than a passing idea; the thought is captured and can be returned to and built upon later. I encourage you to note your 'a-ha', insights, reflections, and the connections you make between ideas or with your context and experience. Also, note your thoughts about where or how you may experiment with the new behaviour and how it worked out when you did.

(2) Travelling Companions: Journeying with one or two other people is often more effective and enjoyable than by oneself. The sharing and discussion of insights and thoughts amplify your own reflection and helps to keep us committed, moving, and improving. Find at least one partner to journey with through the book or select chapters, finding your own tempo and ways to interact virtually or in person.

PART TWO
Aspire

Stand firm on the Purpose, Values and Stakeholder Interests that you choose to represent. 'Aspire' is about having personal goals and values, while 'inspire' is about motivating and Influencing others through actions, words, or achievements. If you don't aspire, how will you inspire others?

What Impact Do You Aspire to Achieve?

'If I were asked to define leadership, I should say it is the "projection of personality". It is the most intensely personal thing in the world because it is just plain you.'

— Field Marshall Viscount Slim

In today's VUCA, post-truth, hyper-dynamic context, it takes courage to stand for something. As the saying goes, 'you can't please everyone all the time'. Whatever course of action you decide upon or decision you take, you can expect either celebration or criticism and complaint that is both intense and unrepresentative. Minority voices of whatever persuasion are amplified disproportionately, particularly by digital media, aided by bots, algorithms and 'likes' (whether real or not). The number of 'likes', the level of media attention and coverage, the passion of extreme supporters or attackers bears little resemblance to the opinion of the majority. You can only lead in this environment if you know what you stand for and won't stand for.

Knowing yourself and the values and ethics you choose to live by have always been important leadership factors, but they are arguably more important today. Why? Because the more dynamic the environment, the greater the level of uncertainty and the speed of change; yet, as leaders, we must take timely decisions. To move forward into the unknown, unfolding future, we must be guided by our values and commitment to the destination we strive to achieve; data only exists on the past.

OL: Leadership is like a person walking across a tightrope – balancing carefully in a blizzard of factors that are constantly buffeting them. The key is the bar they hold–which is labelled 'values'. They must be obvious, authentic, clear, and prepared to be held to account – then, perhaps you can lead successfully.

To lead, you must decide on the direction and intended destination; which needs, causes, people and objectives will you prioritise and, by definition, which you will not be prioritising? The thought leader Michael Porter stated it well when he said, 'strategy is about making choices, what to do and what not to do'. He later described the malaise of managers who spread the available resources across multiple competing initiatives, each insufficiently funded to achieve any substantive impact. He described such an ineffectual approach as a chicken doing 'peck and chase'.

AB: What is different today is that the business leader must not resist change, as many industries did in the past. Every business must proactively question its practices and their impact on customers, employees, and society. You don't wait for a law change to oblige you to do something; you proactively make efforts and commit resources to research and measure if your practices really benefit your stakeholders. You are a catalyst for change to improve society. It is a duty and a smart business decision because it's the way to maximise the value of your company in the long term.

Chapter 2
What's Your Purpose?

Without a Purpose you're just pointing at yourself; why should others follow?

MH1: Purpose – ensure that you connect to staff; through staff, connect to customers. Connect to peers across the organisation, drawing on one another. True purposes sit across organisations, dare I say it, across an entire economy. The purpose should be clear and a bit revolutionary – you must bring your staff. Define the mission; this will allow your people to buy in, and then you are not fighting for their loyalty; instead, they bring in their friends and customers. But this requires a high degree of moral courage.

In the pre-pandemic period, there was already strong evidence that companies pursuing purpose and profit outperformed profit-only enterprises in the medium and long term. During the pandemic, those purpose-led companies outperformed their peers in talent, value, and revenue retention. The benefits of being purpose-led are profound and significant. According to Raj Sisodia, author of *Conscious Capitalism*,[6] Purpose-driven firms in the US produced an outstanding aggregate return of 1,681 per cent over the 15 years pre-pandemic, compared to 118 per cent for the S&P 500. Purpose also sparks innovation and acts as an antidote to short-termism. Simon McKenzie of the Bridge Institute states, 'Purpose is the greatest motivator, more important than compensation, it attracts and retains the best talent, it boosts the brand, increases wellbeing and empowers.'

Through the turmoil of the Covid pandemic and continuing with the erosion of trust and authority of many public and multinational institutions, we are witnessing the rise of voice, passion, and action of purpose-fuelled individuals and enterprises. Protests, civil disobedience, militancy, and accelerated job-hopping challenge the norms and assumptions of the relationship between enterprises and stakeholders – investors, employees, or customers. The shift to purpose-fuelled individuals is profound. Individuals migrate to organisations that align with their point of view on what matters and how people interact or should be treated. There is decreased tolerance for behaviours with which they are uncomfortable. They are changing society by building momentum to causes that they are passionate about, such as Black Lives Matter, # MeToo, and other movements.

The pursuit of purpose is vital for the success of individuals and organisations.[7] Researchers Nick Craig and Scott Snook argue that no developmental task is as critical to leaders as developing their purpose and then taking action to achieve it. Purpose is central to the meaningful life of an organisation or an individual. In the book Built to Last,[8] authors Collins and Porras claim that purpose is an important success factor of outstanding companies. At the centre of product innovation or service excellence is purpose. It has also been demonstrated that a leader's purposefulness is positively and significantly related to their effectiveness.[9] Despite the importance of purpose, most leaders do not have a clear sense of purpose – neither for themselves nor their organisations. Purpose is personal in nature; what motivates you to get out of bed each day – what will give you a buzz of energy to go to work? Purpose is something in you, your role is to discover and develop it, to know whether you are working towards or against it – or ignoring it (for now!)

Purpose: A Constant in a Fast-Changing World

SM: Leaders develop a deep sense of personal purpose. This purpose stands for the greater good of others – it unleashes energy and courage. With a deep sense of personal purpose, leaders recognise it is their role and duty to step forward.

Purposeful leaders stand out. They plant themselves firmly on a cause for which they have more than passion; they have a deeply held belief that is being violated within the status quo and a strong sense of indignation. A strong sense of purpose drives them; they are purpose-fuelled. Simon McKenzie of Bridge Partnership describes such leaders as having the courage to 'step into the "boxing ring", knowing that their opponent is strong and skilled, that they will undoubtedly be punched and bruised and may well be knocked out, but they must do it. Their conviction gives them the courage to step into the ring; it does not remove their fear.'

CS: I think successful leadership begins first with the ability to define with clarity the future that he/she is pursuing and, at the same time, communicate effectively to those he/she leads.

KC: Purpose is so important to an individual.

CS: Leaders should take time to reflect on whether their leadership serves their life's purpose.

TS: You are equipped to pursue your purpose. You need to live in the flow – between your purpose and your capabilities – then you perform at your best. I have a purpose-based approach to my work and, therefore, less stress and self-doubt.

Inspire Others Through Purpose

As individuals have become more aware of societal issues, they have become less tolerant of behaviours that are not aligned with their values and beliefs. They are becoming less willing to follow leaders who do not share those same beliefs and aspirations and want to work with colleagues who share similar goals.

MH: Purpose – will be increasingly important; [people] today are very aware, savvy, and think beyond how to pay for the mortgage.

WS: The sense of purpose is important. People have wanted that for a long time – but now they are prepared to prioritise more about that, rather than salary and other benefits.

AJ: Identify a purpose, and ignite passion and desire in others, to unite them in a way that maximises capacity to achieve lasting and meaningful impact for good. People need to feel a purpose connects them, and the person leading is genuine and authentic – clear on where they want to take people and how they want to make the journey, not just the result.

AW: Each individual must believe in the purpose and that the messaging has only one reason, to push towards said purpose.

DH: The team has all got to understand the mission – and the system by which they come together and collaborate. Purpose is fundamental to this – why are we here, why does this company exist? Even if that purpose is to make money, as long as everyone is aligned.

The Purpose-Fuelled Enterprise

As a leader, to be effective in achieving high impact, there must be alignment between your personal purpose and that of the enterprise. Too often, senior executives pay lip service to the pursuit of the purpose of the enterprise (or may even have been involved in its determination), but they themselves are not personally connected to it. They support relevant initiatives, and hope that the purpose will encourage employee engagement whilst they continue to prioritise their own agenda or short-term operating results. A personal paradigm shift might be required; do you honestly believe, or not, that the pursuit of purpose will positively impact performance and value creation of the enterprise over the mid to long term? You cannot lead effectively in today's context – attracting, inspiring, and retaining followers while navigating unexpected challenges – without embracing and acting in the pursuit of a purpose.

SM: You must become a force for good. Customers will come to you, employees will come to you, and investors will come to you – but you have to be at the front, making a significant difference.

WN: The leader has to hold on tight to the purpose and vision – this is their domain, and they must be the ones setting the direction and keep everyone focused on it – they need to be effective at communicating this – and engaging others on it.

NH: Purpose: makes it not rudderless and an exciting place to work. Our purpose is 'Healthier lives of people through the ingredients we place into foods. Serving the communities where we work. Caring for the planet.' We try to knit these three pillars together. When I became CEO, I wanted to lead the purpose initiative.

CS: When I was CEO at [XXXX], one of the questions that kept coming up in my mind was what should be the organisation's purpose. Given its mandate to operate a lottery monopoly in the country, I felt it had to be more than just an operator. We decided that our purpose must ultimately benefit the community. As such, I started [YYYY], whose purpose is to enable the digital transformation of charities. In the business world, profits must be earned through purpose. Leaders must be able to see how the organisations they lead connect to purposeful outcomes.

RP: Future leaders must provide their employees with a much greater sense of purpose and context. Those employees born after the millennium live in a world where social media platforms democratise opinion, and traditional hierarchies don't stop their voices from being expressed or heard.

Purpose-anchored agility. Knowing the purpose and referring to it helps guide a leader's decisions in otherwise uncertain situations. Knowing why I am here and what I am trying to achieve can reduce the uncertainty and anxiety that come from trying to optimise every decision for short-term gain in a dynamic and volatile context. In the highly dynamic context of today, change and evolution must be constant. Continuous evolution is not only normal; it is essential. However, imposed change processes can create a period of disturbance during which anxiety and ambiguity may undermine performance. The enterprise cannot afford to be continuously underperforming but must be continuously evolving. An alternative approach is to involve employees throughout the enterprise to initiate and drive change in the pursuit of purpose. Changes cease to be lurches between alternative management plans but necessary agility and improvements in pursuit of the purpose.

CM: [We need] tolerance and expectation that vision can/will be flexed over time. People who are more tolerant of leaders evolving their thinking. Leaders who are confident in themselves are more comfortable allowing themselves to be challenged and, therefore, freer to let their thinking evolve. These guys will do well in today's environment, whereas those who are more rigid will struggle.

NH: You must have real clarity of direction. New shocks will always be coming; we need to be agile in the short term. It's a hard-lived experience for your workforce – so you need to give people clarity on where you are going. [You need] ambition, excitement on where you are taking the company, to ensure that they stay with you while battling short-term issues [...]. You need to be able to tell stories about the progress that you are making towards the longer goals while being honest about the short-term issues.

Find Your Purpose

Some may have had personal experiences that significantly disrupted the way they view the world and their place in it. For others, an area of interest and affinity may have quietly lain dormant in their life and emotions to date. I have always enjoyed being around horses. Not that I could afford to act on it growing up as a teenager,

I was lucky if I was gifted a riding lesson once a year. However, the older and more successful in business I became, the more I could indulge my interest in horses, even going as far as buying a farm (as a hobby) and converting it from cattle to horse breeding and training. Whenever possible, I would be on a horse riding the hills, forests, and rivers. Slowly I began to realise that the thing I loved most about the horses was being out in nature with them. Yes, they were fun to ride, but not riding in the arena, being out with the eagles, the snakes, and the kangaroos. This notion festered within me for a few more years until I eventually left the career behind and established a company that would connect busy city-based executives to a patch of glorious nature through interactions with horses. My purpose was to raise advocacy for and investment in the environment through the enjoyment of nature. I targeted the population of influential and wealthy executives and celebrities, as they would have the most influence. I then configured our offerings to be relevant and attractive for these people.

Discovering your purpose requires finding the overlapping point of three questions (Figure 2.1). The process can be undertaken as an individual or collectively by the leadership team of an enterprise.

1. **Passion:** What motivates you? What do you care deeply about?
   - My passion: I loved spending time with horses, particularly riding in nature.

2. **Societal need:** What's the bigger picture? What is it about society now that is in the way of your passion? What are you indignant about – what needs to be changed?
   - Causes that matter to me: (1) Appreciation of and need to protect the environment, (2) Stress management and wellbeing.

3. **Talents and strengths:** What skills, assets, relationships, or experiences do you have that you could leverage to make a difference?
   - My strengths and unique capabilities: (1) Strategy and Business Model Design, (2) Client Relationship Management and Networks, (3) Horse Farm and Skilled Staff.

Figure 2.1

SM: The purpose is to lead for the betterment of humanity and the planet. Real leaders believe they exist for a higher purpose: to better the lives of others– [in a] heartfelt [way]. The purpose is at the centre.

The Primacy of Meaning and Purpose

There is broad awareness of the importance of addressing major societal issues (such as those defined in the United Nations Sustainable Development Goals). There is also research demonstrating that purposeful organisations outperform (in terms of shareholder value creation) those that are purely for-profit and that such enterprises are better able to attract, retain and motivate talent. However, in 2020 it was estimated that fewer than 10,000 enterprises globally were purpose-led. A growing number of organisations centre themselves on a purposeful mission, in part as a response to the issues they seek to address and in part in response to pressure from the talent marketplace.

DH: DEI and ESG are super important now – so maybe there will be a new class of leaders who can master this context. We will see fewer firms [from the West] trying to impose their values on businesses and governments elsewhere. Currently, so many Western firms and media seem to think that they have the right to demand that other nations have Western values – you saw this in the World Cup in Qatar –media, teams and fans thought that they should dictate what the rules and values of this Islamic country should be. There will be greater tolerance, understanding and inclusion in the future.

MH2: You're not going to be in business if you don't do something about environmental sustainability; there will be increasing civil unrest about it. Also, at the World Economic Forum this year, there was a big emphasis on the erosion of social cohesion. That means [more people] fighting and falling apart.

SW: I think we will see more leaders standing up and being vocal and visible about change – [as opposed to current] leaders within organisations who may or may not urge change. I think we will see more leaders creating businesses that are different, overtaking and replacing the corporations that are only adjusting slowly – think of Tesla vs General Motors.

Pause, Reflect and Experiment: What's Your Purpose?

(1) What are you passionate about?
- What makes you cry, jump for joy, energises you or makes you angry when you see it?
- What evidence is there at present or in the past that you are truly passionate about these things; what have you done?

(2) Is there a bigger societal need associated with the issues that you are passionate about?
- What is the overarching theme within which you find and express your passions?
- Does this theme echo or align with any of the United Nations Sustainable Development Goals?

(3) What are you good at doing or enjoy doing that can be applied and that you could direct and develop in service of the topic you are passionate about?
- Do you have – or can you build – credibility and strengthen these capabilities, e.g., qualifications, recognition by others, impact stories, and testimonials?

(4) If you are unsure about where to start looking, then these simple and effective steps can be the following:

- **UN SDG:** Look at the 17 Sustainable Development Goals[10] that the United Nations adopted in 2015. Spending even a short while reading a little about each of these goals and the challenges now being faced will trigger your thoughts and emotions about which areas inspire you more.
- **Purpose safari:** Another approach is that you can join in or conduct your own 'purpose safari'. In small groups, visit places and meet representatives of those impacted by different factors while being guided in reflection by a coach. Depending on the budget and focus, we've met with migrants at refugee camps and with victims of female trafficking; seen and discussed deforestation with villagers, loggers and the government; visited orphanages and monasteries; scooped up plastic waste in the oceans and of course, explored nature under stress in different areas of the world.

(5) When you have even an ember of interest in one or other area, be it in line with an SDG or not, then reach out to and connect with individuals or organisations that are active in that space. Hundreds (if not thousands) of individuals and organisations are active in most areas. Connect with a few, subscribe to their channel or newsfeeds, turn up to an event or two and try to speak to them directly. From any of these simple first steps, you will see what inspires you personally, and you can then decide whether and how to engage more actively. I don't recommend following my model of quitting your job and moving to another country to pursue the mission unless you have done more exploration and planning than I did. Although not having a 'plan B' did focus my mind and efforts, I discovered much greater resourcefulness and resilience than I had imagined – and eventually, it worked out!

(6) Bring purpose to life.

- What is the vision that you have for the outcome that you want to see?
- What do you envisage you will be doing (and the impact you are having) in 3–5 years if you live out your purpose?
- To reach the 3–5 years' vision, what will you do in 1–2 years?
- To reach the 1–2 years' vision, what will you do in 6 months?
- To reach the 6-month vision, what do you need to be doing now and over the next three months?

Panel Views: Being Purpose-Fuelled

Below I have included comments from several leaders who indicate where their passion or indignation lies and where you, too, may find the embers of a purpose that you wish to ignite.

NH: I believe in big external events sparking change in the company. Consider Greta Thunberg's rise in popularity for saying climate change has happened, not that it is happening – this triggered me to bring environmental issues into the company's heart. Also, George Floyd's death supported a massive acceleration in our thinking on DEI. I had set goals for gender equality before then – but traction got going after George Floyd – it became OK to have a conversation about the topic.

CE: There are inflexion points – e.g., learnings from the actions during the pandemic. In education, we have learned a lot about remote learning – how it has marginalised many individuals, particularly all those who did not have the means to continue remotely (600 million children globally). We need to learn and build back better – e.g., learning without exams. It's highlighted more strongly who the stakeholders really are – the kids are key stakeholders – whom we haven't listened to or thought holistically about before. We need to be more sensitive to these stakeholders – thinking about their mental and social wellbeing, not just their exam results. The role of education is much broader.

TS: I have become something – and now young, black women in [Latin America] are a part of my stakeholder group that I care about and for whom I do things – I am an example for them. I had to accept wearing that responsibility. It has transformed even my sense of happiness. Others in authority around me may not care about these groups – but I do.

TC: The influence of environmental challenges is increasingly important in my world of investment and banking; we are continually faced by our customer base expecting us to be aware of responsible investing and sustainability. We have the governance in place (in the reporting we put forward), so it's inevitable that it feeds into and weaves across all roles: the way that we conduct our business. It's increasingly obvious when a manager is not operating with an awareness of environmental issues or responsibility for sustainability and good governance. It's becoming like when somebody lights up a cigarette. It used to be commonplace if you went to the pub and saw somebody smoking; now, it's out of place, and it's much the same with environmental issues. It's increasingly important to convey concern, awareness and actions about responsible investing, sustainability and the cost-of-living challenge.

WN: ESG – it's on the agenda of every CEO. They must have a response to and a position on this. Regulation insists on it. Customers insist on it (both B2B and B2C). Competitors are acting. So, there's pressure to step up. Financiers are also applying pressure. Decarbonisation is the main focus. Davos spent a whole session talking about ESG. It's real – it's here now – you must respond now – you must have a viewpoint. The Ukraine War will lead to less reliance on fossil fuels – as a reaction against reliance on Russia. On a personal level, I have switched over in the past eight months; now, I have solar at home and EV cars plugged in at work.

BH: Compare 1922 to 2022 – now we know that enterprises do not take care of society. There was a need to revolutionise society 100 years ago - and also now. We have to change how we think about society. We must be cooperatively community-based. We cannot be solely market-based – we must focus on community and cooperate to build society. Enterprises cannot do this without a top-down government imposition and a deeply held set of beliefs and actions by individuals – this is what I am trying to influence.

Chapter 3
What Values Do You Stand For?

Your values are defined by what you walk by or let slide;
not by what you tell yourself.

BH: Values are incredibly important – [and] the ability to articulate those values. Before, you had a core set of values, and that was enough – no longer; now, you must be able to communicate them authentically, make them visible, make them apparent – and live and say them consistently. Any inconsistency will be put back to you. It is hard, as the decisions you are being asked to make are increasingly difficult.

The values you stand for are much more visible today, facilitated by social media and demanded by direct and indirect stakeholders. It has always been important to know and consistently stand on values to be successful as a leader, but in today's context, it is inescapable. Inconsistency between how you actually behave and what you claim to promote will become visible. A recent example in the mainstream media revealed a culture of bullying and misogyny whilst overtly promoting gender diversity and inclusion.

You must know your values rather than those that sound good or that you think might be appropriate for an audience to hear. If you have yet to stand on a value in the face of pressure or inconvenience, then you probably don't know if it really matters to you and defines you or it just something that you would like to be associated with. It's not what you tell yourself are the values that matter to you; what defines you is what you stand for, what you walk by, let pass or tell yourself 'Not here. Not now. Not yet'. What you don't do is often as visible to others as what you do; your actions define your persona in the eyes of others.

While ethics are often assumed to be 'universal' standards (although heavily influenced by culture and religion), values can be entirely personal; they vary from one person to the next. Whereas one person might highly value transparency (for example, 'we now have more data and therefore need to change the decision'), another may prioritise certainty and consistency (for example, 'just stick with contract/original scope of work; let's get through this first stage and then if necessary, discuss a possible phase 2'). Thus, two individuals may behave differently even when pursuing the same purpose and sharing a similar cultural view of ethics. Leaders must know the values they will stand for; what they will not compromise on. To trust you, followers need to know your values and see that you consistently act accordingly, especially when in a situation which has high stakes or high ambiguity. A leader whose life is guided by values and principles is a leader with moral authority;[11] imbued with trust and respected.

Values-based Leaders Are More Effective

In the past few decades values-based leadership (VBL) has become a well-known topic of academic research. VBL wasn't extensively studied previously; as such, it is impossible to say whether it has always been the case that values-based leaders have produced better outcomes or, indeed, whether, in previous times, most leaders' approaches were values-based. This century, the topic became the focus of attention due to the rising visibility of corporate and political failure cases where leadership was evidently not values-based. (For example, Enron, Anderson, WorldCom, Volkswagen, Theranos, Uber, and several financial institutions at the centre of the global financial crisis).

The research of this century has illuminated a clear truth: in our current context, the four primary models of values-based leadership – (1) servant[12] (2) transformational[13] (3) authentic[14] and (4) ethical[15] leadership – all lead to superior long-term corporate performance outcomes. These models of leadership, grounded in strong values, prove to be exceptionally effective. While each model emphasizes distinct virtues and behaviours, they also share common ground.

The domain of values-based leadership research gained recognition in the 1970s. Key research papers on servant leadership[16] and transformational leadership[17] emerged in 1977 and 1978, marking significant milestones. Bill George's 2003 book,[18] underlines the power of leaders who lead with purpose, values, and integrity, creating lasting organisations that motivate employees to deliver exceptional customer service and generate enduring shareholder value.

In their 2005 article titled 'Diagnosing and Changing Organizational Culture',[19] Cameron and Quinn encapsulate the impact of values-based leadership on individuals within an organisation at multiple levels. This impact extends from physiological benefits such as improved health, to emotional benefits like resistance to depression, and psychological benefits including enhanced memory. Moreover, they extend the effects to the organizational level, affirming that companies grounded in values-based leadership exhibit greater profitability, heightened productivity, improved quality, and elevated satisfaction levels among both employees and customers.

Servant Leadership

At the core of servant leadership lies a leader's consideration of others' desires, a dedication to developing and empowering followers, and the prioritisation of followers' needs over their own. Such leaders are driven by a genuine desire to serve. They are defined by traits such as unwavering moral character, the skill of nurturing relationships and uplifting others, strong leadership attributes coupled with a willingness to guide, an eagerness to enhance organisational processes, and a role-model status that strives to make a positive impact on society and culture.

Transformational Leadership

Transformational leadership unfolds as a process that positively affects both leader and follower, consequently enhancing organisational outcomes. Embedded within this approach are ethical and moral components. Transformational leaders are described as those who tap into the moral values of their subordinates, inspiring them to instigate change and elevate their organisations.

Authentic Leadership

Authentic leadership embodies a leader's resolute sense of purpose, a genuine approach to leading, a robust ethical and moral compass, the ability to foster genuine connections, and the display of self-discipline and restraint. Authentic leaders possess self-awareness, harnessing their values, moral perspective, knowledge, and strengths to lead effectively. Followers recognize them as embodiments of confidence, hope, optimism, resilience, and moral character. For a deeper dive into authentic leadership, recommended reads include *True North*[20] by Bill George and *On Becoming a Leader*[21] by Warren Bennis.

Ethical Leadership

Ethics, as universally understood values that transcend cultural boundaries, hold immense significance. While only a handful of values genuinely pass this universal test, ethical leaders are those who exemplify altruism, honesty, empathy, empowerment, fairness, and justice. They uphold principles of fairness and high integrity, thereby fostering followers' confidence and trust in them.

JA: Leaders [must] have a firm and deep connection to their core values and purpose. I would argue that successful leader makes their decisions based on their values. Without a clear understanding of their values, a leader will become paralysed by indecision, inconsistent in response, and generally ineffective at the times when leadership is most needed.

Panel Views: Know the Values That You Will Stand For

This section highlights the four most frequently cited values by the panel during our interviews.

---

(1) Moral Courage   (2) Integrity   (3) Selflessness   (4) Humility

---

Moral Courage

Moral courage is the fortitude to stand for what you believe to be ethical and right despite the pressures that you believe you are facing to do otherwise.

KC: Leadership without a moral compass is not leadership.

BH: You must not shy away from the challenges and opportunities that come your way. See the things around you. Are you trying to get through the year or looking to make a difference? I hold tightly to the expression, 'The standard that you walk past is the standard you promote' ... Do you choose to see what is happening and to do something about it – or do you 'turn a blind eye' or shy away from it?

MH: Moral courage is essential in leadership – and, I would say, in all decent human beings.

PM: Moral courage is the greatest of the virtues – great moral courage. It means [having] a moral compass that is perfectly set and the courage to use it to make decisions – which is getting harder, partly because society is getting more litigious. Great leaders get it about right very quickly. Listen to advice and get on with it. What do leaders do? They decide, which requires courage as there is always uncertainty and ambiguity.

OL: [courage] has always been important, but it is more important now that you know your values. The highest is moral courage. Courage is not only a virtue; it is THE virtue, as it is the virtue from which all others flow.

Integrity

Integrity is being honest and adhering to strong moral and ethical principles; this leads to consistent behaviours that inspire trust.

HW: Fundamental to any leader is to have and be known for integrity; without integrity, there cannot be trust, and without trust, no one follows you.

MH: The integrity to stand up and be counted. For me, it has always been this way. But I know this is not matched in wider society – and most people are not leaders.

OL: You should be prepared to walk away from any situation, any organisation where your integrity might be compromised. Guard your integrity fiercely; once lost, it might never be recovered.

Selflessness: Care for Others

Caring more about the needs and wants of others than your own; being prepared to sacrifice your own goals or comforts to support others in attaining theirs.

AK: The ability to demonstrate authentic compassion builds relationships, builds trust and the credibility of the leader.

EB: Be selfless, really caring for the greater good; [you need the] ability to shape opinions and inspire people to take action

JH: Reduce your ego, as it should not be about you first but the employees, customers, and consumers you serve.

NH: Care is interesting, as people are drawn to and inspired by a leader that they think has got their backs. The root of trust (which is so important) is the belief that you have their back.

OL: [The] keyword is care – for your people, the organisation, and the environment, [display] selflessness and humility; do the right thing, and don't walk on by. It's not about you.

Humility

Humility is the absence of pride or arrogance. A humble person is receptive to alternative perspectives, respectful of others and open to learning.

AB: Be humble: The moment you think you don't need other people's opinions, you will make the most dangerous career mistake.

SG: The key is the ability to be humble in this and to integrate and orchestrate conversations … I think the new normal is a kind of humility.

RB: More people today are aware of their limits. As a day-to-day operating principle, the value of intellectual humility is really powerful. However, people often learn this need for humility the hard way, through a major mistake or failure.

MH: Humility – accept that not you, your organisation, or your team have it all right. Admit where we have made mistakes. Learn, admit, and commit, then act – move ahead. [You need] humility around your historical performance – don't pretend you have always done everything right.

PC: More people today know the limits of their brilliance and knowledge. The value of intellectual humility as a day-to-day operating principle; is really powerful. Leaders need to ask the right questions – more so than provide the answers – and the humility to listen to the answers given. The more I know, the greater my awareness of how little I know.

Pause, Reflect and Experiment: What Values Will You Stand For?

(1) What are the values that you intensely care about? Can you describe an actual situation where you have stood on the values you care about that risked or resulted in significant negative consequences?
  • Take a long list of values (Note: a list is included in the Appendix) and highlight the ones you think are extremely important to you.
  • From the list you highlighted, create a rank order in which no two values can have the same ranking.
  • Looking at the top 5 values – write down the last time you have stood on that value when under pressure or tempted to do otherwise.

(2) Who are your role models (now or growing up), and why?
  • For each person, what is (or what was) it about them that inspired you? What values do they embody (in your version of your story about them)?

- Look across the lists of values that you have identified associated with the different people you have held as a role model. What are the most common shared values or themes?
- Look at the top 5 values – write down the last time you have stood on that value when under pressure to conform or agree with perceived group norms.

(3) How will you hold yourself accountable to always stand on the identified short-list of 3–5 values in all areas of your life, in the quiet hidden spaces and when visible to others?

- Create reminders of the prioritised values and why they matter to you (e.g., images of your role models, statements of the values and why they matter to you).
- Declare your values to others (e.g., referring to one or other specific value in a communication).
  - Anticipate and welcome that others will hold you to account for living by your declared values.
- When confronted by a difficult situation – pause, think about how to apply the values.
- Write down when you stand on your declared values or compromise them.

Chapter 4
What Are You Responsible for, to Whom Are You Accountable?

You can't please everyone all the time.
Decide who and what you are responsible for.

OL: At the heart of Responsible Leadership is recognising that everything is more important than you are. You are in the service of what you are trying to achieve and those you lead to achieve that. I'm a believer that the leader 'eats last'.[22]

What Is Responsible Leadership – And Why Does It Matter?

Leadership is about doing the right thing, whereas 'management' is doing things right. As very few people set out to be 'irresponsible', as such, why does 'leadership' need to be preceded by the adjective 'responsible'. As a term, 'responsible leadership' has appeared in literature and business media for over 70 years. The origins of responsible leadership can, however, be traced further back, including the exploration of virtue and moral character in Confucian and Socratic philosophies approximately 2,500 years ago. Yet unfortunately, as discussed in the opening section, there are, and have been, multiple examples of 'poor' leadership, including corporate, government and NGO/charity scandals.

BL: Responsible leadership is doing the right thing well.

MH: Responsible leadership is doing the right thing, not just doing things right.

Since 1952 there has been discussion and celebration of the intent for responsible leadership. Milton Friedman and Peter Drucker both articulated the corporation's role as being responsible for the well-being and prosperity of the societies in which they operate in order to propagate the conditions for their continuing success. Marx and Lenin said that the state and not the corporation should be responsible for the same reason.

BJ: Drucker wrote about responsibility in the 1950s. If firms don't apply this, they will be 'f*****', as no one will want to work for them. Most people in their 20s [and 30s] want to work for a positive-impact, mission-driven organisation. But the concept has been around for 70 years; the difference is that now it's risen to the top of more people's consciousness – this issue of responsibility is now front and centre.

Kofi Annan (the 7th Secretary General of the United Nations) brought attention to responsible leadership, particularly through his speeches in 2005 and 2006. In an interview in 2014, he stated, 'People want responsible leadership. On big issues, they are not going to sit in their homes. They will act and press for action [moving] from value to values, from shareholders to stakeholders, and from balance sheets to balanced development'.[23] More recently, the World Economic Forum's 'Davos Revolution' states, 'The purpose of a company is to engage all its stakeholders in shared and sustained value creation. In creating such value, a company serves not only its shareholders but all its stakeholders – employees, customers, suppliers, local communities, and society at large.'[24] Accenture reflected this broad perspective in its Five Elements Model of Responsible Leadership[25] that it promoted at the time of the Davos summit. The five elements are:

- **Stakeholder Inclusion:** Safeguarding trust and positive impact for all by standing in the stakeholders' shoes when making decisions and fostering an inclusive environment where diverse individuals have a voice and feel they belong.

- **Emotion and Intuition:** Unlocking commitment and creativity by being truly human, showing compassion, humility and openness.

- **Mission and Purpose:** Advancing common goals by inspiring a shared vision of sustainable prosperity for the organisation and its stakeholders.

- **Technology and Innovation:** Creating new organisational and societal value by innovating responsibly with emerging technology.

- **Intellect and Insight:** Finding ever-improving paths to success by embracing continuous learning and knowledge exchange.

These holistic, inclusive perspectives on responsible leadership are undoubtedly well-intentioned; the challenge is how to be responsible for everything all the time. As observers, it may be easy to point to errors and missteps retrospectively or to amplify the voice of minority groups who may feel overlooked or otherwise aggrieved. However, this does not always mean the leader has acted irresponsibly – it might just be that no person, leader or not, can be accountable to everyone and all their competing needs.

MH: The big difficulty of responsible leadership is 'responsible to whom, for what?' Nobody is going to say, 'I don't believe in responsible leadership; I believe in irresponsible leadership'! Nobody on the planet is going to say that. So, the difficulty with the phrase is, 'What the heck does it mean?'

So where is the boundary between good and poor leadership, between responsible and irresponsible leadership? Legal frameworks help define some of the 'out-of-bounds' areas, where behaviour is clearly defined as irresponsible but are insufficient either to ensure compliance or to define what is responsible behaviour. My definition of Responsible Leadership is:

"Knowingly acting only in ways that seek to achieve the betterment of the enterprise's stakeholders over the long term".

This necessitates:

(1) Prioritising between the competing claims of various stakeholders (you can't please everyone),

(2) Deciding how to act in pursuit of these claims (you can't do everything), and

(3) Inviting governance oversight from representatives of those stakeholder groups.

I include the word 'knowingly' in my definition as, given the speed of evolution and disruption in today's context, we cannot know the future and must make the best decisions we can at any given moment. I also emphasise long- rather than short-term, as it is important to avoid seeking to optimise for immediate gain at the expense of longer-term strength, impact or survival. However, even with the best intent and robust practices, as 'we can't please everyone all the time' and we 'can't do everything', and we are making choices without data on the future, there is still the risk of an unseen situation flaring up for which we are not prepared. In hindsight, it might therefore be said we had not been responsible. Of course, even if a leader embraces the above definition of being responsible, there is no guarantee that the enterprise will succeed!

BJ: Good leaders are responsible. Irresponsible leaders are poor leaders, although they are still leaders and may achieve the outcomes they want.

Often the rationale put forward for responsible leadership is to avoid scandals and collapses of the type mentioned previously. However, this is the weakest argument, as scandals depend on some misstep being discovered and successfully prosecuted. The rationale for being responsible as a leader is that it is only through doing so that we can achieve a lasting positive impact on society, for us and our children. It's the right thing to do. In 1984, management thought leader Peter Drucker wrote the paper 'The New Meaning of Corporate Social Responsibility', arguing that businesses should NOT be exploitative entities that then benevolently give money to suitable socially 'good' causes. Instead, he argued that 'the proper social responsibility of business is to 'turn a social problem into economic opportunity and economic benefit into productive capacity, human competence, well-paid jobs and wealth'. Or, in other words, 'Do good to do well' – a sentiment reflected in my work on purpose-fuelled entities.

AI: It's easy to 'greenwash', but successful businesses take responsible leadership seriously. Responsible leadership must be good for the business and play to the strengths of the organisation – so it's NOT about sending your staff to paint fences for a school! Use the organisation's core skills to make a positive impact – in line with your business objective.

PC1: Responsible business – the need for businesses to step up and be responsible has never been greater. Government regulation cannot keep up with the pace of change.

EB: Responsible leadership is about caring for the greater good and for the impact of those that your enterprise touches (directly or indirectly).

Responsible Leadership Has 'Come of Age'

IS: The term 'responsible leadership' has come of age – but is rather idiosyncratic, dependent on individual leaders' preferences and biases. There is a crisis of capitalism. Individuals have been financially rewarded for short-term performance that has not looked after the interests of many stakeholders, even allowing them to be exploited; it's been highly transactional.

SW: Talking about responsible leadership is now possible, whereas previously, while I tried to act responsibly, I would not have brought it to the attention of the board of directors or the investors. Now I can shape the debate on some policies I want us to adopt with the language of being responsible and the reputational risk of not adopting them.

Whilst the relevancy or concept of responsible leadership remains distant to many organisations, stakeholders and leaders, the philosophy is no longer on the periphery of management thinking or practice. The desire of many leaders and stakeholders to promote societal issues has found its voice, garners attention and is increasingly embedded into governance structures and processes. Equally, the personal and corporate costs of scandals linked to failures to lead responsibly are further fuelling efforts to act and to be seen to act in ways deemed to be responsible.

SG: This is potentially one of those moments where the barriers that used to exist for a business to fulfil its true role have disappeared, but not everyone has noticed yet. So many are still kind of trucking along in the same group. But gradually, more people are looking around. The investors saying, 'I don't give a crap about ESG, show me the money', are dwindling. So are the customers who say, 'I just want that super snazzy brand even though they employ slaves'. Show me the employees who get paid the money and dedicate themselves to only their working life, regardless of the organisation's purpose. A contingent [of people like that] might exist forever, but they're getting smaller and smaller. This is a progression towards a rediscovery of what business is for; serving people and our planet. There will undoubtedly be blips along the way, but I think it's unstoppable.

JA: I wrote an article following the killing of George Floyd and the televised protests that ensued, as many businesses engaged in what I would describe as virtue signalling about how terrible the killing of Mr Floyd was. As a father of an African American young man in Chicago, I worried both for his safety and what leaders from across the spectrum were actively doing to voice support and actively engage as part of a solution. I see that business leaders – who collectively control trillions of dollars in products, commerce, and services, have a corporate and moral obligation to shareholders, their consumers, and partners to be a positive and active force in the engagement of these social, civic and environmental issues that impact society and the planet.

Greater Transparency: Nowhere to Hide

Increasingly, awareness is growing that irresponsible behaviour will likely be discovered. Also, the damage to the enterprise and the individuals involved is likely to be severe; judicial proceedings are more frequent, fines are increasing, reputational damage has a lasting impact. It would be wonderful to think that leaders are also acting more responsibly for more altruistic reasons; however, as several of the comments below indicate, many remain sceptical that that is the primary driver.

SG: I think several things are different now; I think the asset owners are awake to the impact of what their capital does, and they're taking a more active interest in what the asset managers do with their money. They are connected generationally, so their grandkids, who might otherwise in times past have sat meekly at dinner and thanked them for the bursary, are now going, 'How do you feel about our money going towards X company?', 'What has company so and so done', etc. That pressure from the younger generation isn't going to go away.

I don't believe that the idealists of the Greta Thunberg generation will grow up to be cynical 40–50 somethings saying, 'Just show me the money; I don't care about anyone'. I just don't believe it.

KC: I think there has been a huge rise in the language around responsible leadership – and then business schools (and others) have promoted it – but not in ways that have inculcated [belief]. I think that most of the efforts have failed. Most 'leaders' are not acting in ways that are responsible for all the stakeholder groups [that] their organisation impacts ... Leadership is not easy; it requires you to be responsible for the impact and treatment of the stakeholders. It's called leadership; otherwise, you are just an executive.

CE: The label [responsible leadership] doesn't help – as no one sets out to be irresponsible. There's just good and bad leadership. Good leadership seeks to do good for all stakeholders and create enduring organisations. Irresponsible leaders may seek to optimise outcomes for some at the expense of others, or they may seek to optimise outcomes today without much concern for the future of the enterprise. They are just poor leaders.

Accountable: Deciding Who You Are Accountable To

The fundamental difficulty with the notion of responsible leadership is prioritising between stakeholders and between the multitude of needs and objectives. When a leader takes on their role, they are responsible for the outcomes achieved, which will be judged differently by the various stakeholder groups. A narrow definition of the stakeholders that the leader is accountable to might include employees, customers, and investors, whereas a broader definition might include networks of suppliers and collaborators or society more broadly. Over the past 20 years, there has been increasing pressure to prioritise the needs and desires of indirect stakeholders, enshrined in government policies and lobbied for by media and public opinion. Thus, responsible leadership is increasingly understood to imply that the leader is accountable for the outcomes, impact, and experiences of broader networks of stakeholders, including society and the environment.

RP: Responsible leadership is to be aware of wider stakeholders, interest groups, and communities who have a direct or indirect relationship with the business and to ensure investors, markets, and shareholders all benefit from the value generated by the business. The key evolution of this paradigm is that indirect stakeholders have no direct contractual or business relationship with a company but hold real or perceived vested interests that need to be first acknowledged and then acted upon.

TC: Since the financial crisis of the late noughties, our [financial services] organisation has changed; we're very clear that our membership is our customers; we are accountable to them, so doing the right thing is critical. Our role is to be fair and to understand what fairness is.

Leadership occurs in the relationship between the leader and the stakeholders. Employees can leave, investors can pull back, customers can switch allegiance, suppliers can boycott, and governments can apply penalties if they do not agree with the behaviours or outcomes achieved by the leader and their enterprise. The researchers Thomas Maak and Nicola Pless say, 'Responsible leadership is about building and sustaining trustful relationships with relevant stakeholders'. The most important question is, who are the most relevant stakeholders for the leader? The first choices the leader has to make are between all the stakeholder groups, direct and indirect and between their multiple and often competing objectives. Which stakeholders will the leader be accountable to? Which of their objectives should the leader then prioritise and which to deprioritise?

AW: To truly lead and be sustainable [in the long term], all members must feel they are doing the right thing: that almost all parties are catered for, not just those who can help you. In business, this could prove tricky; however, word of mouth and reputation supersedes profitability in the short term.

PC1: We have to be responsible to a broad set of stakeholders – wider than before. But that said, a responsible leader must first look after their own people. The key responsibility we have is to our people – the employees.

KH: Be open and authentic about who the investors are that you are representing. To have the license to lead, you must be delivering on what the investors want – while recognising that you also are one of those investors, you are investing your time, passion and skills.

SG: [During the pandemic] suddenly, there was the realisation of the impact that the business has on all these other organisations and people as individuals. This became really apparent, and therefore, that sense of responsibility for anything that this organisation decides is going to have an impact. Suddenly there was the realisation that you need to get the opinion of those who will be impacted before you make the decision.

Being Accountable and Acting Responsibly

What is clear is that the turbulent, dynamic context of today is continually testing leaders, requiring timely decisions as the unknown, uncertain future unfolds. While no leader will get every decision 'right', those who do not act in ways that address the needs of prominent stakeholder groups, fail to deliver the results expected or are not anchored on values and ethics will quickly be exposed. This is the era when leadership that is not 'responsible' has fewer places to hide.

TM: Attention to the notion of responsible leadership has been rising – but we have had benign conditions for a long time – since 2008/9. The movement may well lose momentum when we are amid a recession, high unemployment and a cost-of-living crisis. We are already seeing signs of the passion diminishing as growth has slowed and global tensions have risen.

JV: Direct stakeholders set the context for you as a leader – so listen to them first. As a leader, you need to decide which groups you will be prioritising and which issues you will focus on – and then be consistent. Be thoughtful; you may adjust but you can't always please everyone.

PL: A clear focus on encouraging strong performance should always be kept centre-mind. [The] interests of indirect or direct stakeholders must also be kept in mind, of course, but not become sources of performance excuses.

RB: Most CEOs say they would like to act with more holistic responsibility, but the board will not allow us to. Even major global investment funds that spout the importance of sustainable investments are now saying that there is an unacceptably high 'green premium' making investments into ESG-exemplary businesses unattractive, so they must invest elsewhere as well.

The context matters the owners matter – as leaders, we usually respond to what these forces demand; we can't take an independent stance even if we say we are doing so. We all know people who fly in executive jets to Davos to explain their commitment to climate initiatives. So, I think there is a lot more talk than actual action.

More Than One 'Right Answer' or No 'Right' Answer?

The leader makes a choice, implicitly or explicitly, about the stakeholder groups to whom they most feel accountable. How they prioritise the conflicting needs of these different groups will determine their choices in leading the enterprise. As such, any two leaders, believing they are acting responsibly, with high moral values and ethical orientation, will still probably decide different ways to navigate the turbulence, challenges and opportunities they face. Only in hindsight will it be possible to determine whether either, both, or neither of them has been responsible or, rather, is perceived in hindsight to have acted responsibly.

TS: As [my country's] ambassador, who am I serving? This is important. It is a choice to decide which stakeholder groups I am most representing. I realise that I am not representing the Prime Minister; I am representing the people of my country. There are so many potential stakeholder groups within the people of my country – so I still have to see which ones I am really representing. This choice is important for all leaders to recognise. As a leader, you make choices – you can't equally represent everyone all the time. The leader makes choices – knowingly or unknowingly. This step is very important in defining the identity of the leader. What is my self-identity? Why do I have the right to be here in this role? Who am I accountable to?

CS: [It's essential to have] a strong and stable capacity for self-awareness guided by a strong sense of what is right and good for the people and community.

PM: There are thousands of man-made laws – that sometimes need to be broken by the leader that stands up for the moral laws with judgement and courage.

[...] We need to rebuild our moral compass – this is a major challenge facing society. How do we build/rebuild a moral compass in people? We cannot address the problems in society unless we rebuild this. Sometimes leaders will have to be morally right, albeit doing legally wrong things, which will take courage; only then will they make the changes society needs.

SG: Responsible leadership links to ethics, morals and values, which can be at odds with the objectives and behaviours of the company or company culture as lived. Most people think they are there to be responsible and to act with morals and ethics – but somehow, we drift away from this.

Influencer or Responsible?

Leaders are public figures who are both influencers of and in service to a very broad range of stakeholders, including, in some cases, the general public. As such, increasingly, leaders are expected to make public statements on unfolding events, even those that lie outside the scope of knowledge or experience of the leader and the enterprise. Once business leaders kept away from commenting on political and societal issues or emergent stories in the news, now they are increasingly expected to have an opinion and share it publicly. With 24-hour news and 'always-on' social media, modern leaders can no longer content themselves with just running their businesses within their metaphorical 'walls'.

DH: The abnormal is that before, businesspeople have largely tried to stay out of politics – but now it is clear that you can't – you must have an opinion, you must be aware, you must react and manage. How do you manage stakeholder activism and geopolitics? These have come out of left field.

RB: The geopolitical dimensions of leadership cannot be ignored. By contrast, previous business leaders often believed they didn't have to have an opinion on or respond to geopolitical developments. You may not need to know how to figure this stuff out for yourself – but you do need someone in your top team who does. How does the firm respond? Some firms have to split themselves into two (or more now), e.g., China and ex-China, e.g., red states vs blue states in the US.

RS: Focusing on internal issues and results is no longer 'good enough'. In the past, leaders could immerse themselves in their industry, firm, and people. The leader of the future must be adept in understanding global issues:

political, social, environmental, technological, economic, legal, etc., not only to understand but also to develop positions for the firm and navigate the complexity of these factors on a global scale. Perhaps future leaders must have some training in sociology, political economics, and global risk management, as well as an MBA.

Is Too Much Discussion of Responsible Leadership Counterproductive?

An overwhelming sentiment from the leaders who contributed their thoughts to this book is that too much talk about Responsible Leadership is unhelpful. While it has been good to raise the topic and awareness, the distinction between what is defined as Responsible Leadership and what is good leadership is a little abstract. While the core intent of being and acting responsibly is essential, perhaps the Responsible Leadership 'movement' is starting to be counterproductive. Two rationales support such thinking.

(1) The first idea is that the 'label' of being responsible or not can create the conditions whereby leaders are easily accused of being 'irresponsible', even when they have acted rationally, having made careful choices between courses of action, stakeholder groups and possible objectives. The future is unknown, and not everything and everyone can be equally prioritised; this does not mean that the leader has been irresponsible if the outcomes desired by some of the stakeholders are not achieved.

> **JV:** The movement of responsible leadership has become like a woke bandwagon. The rhetoric is now harming the intent. As a leader, I can only chase a few things; I have to make choices and prioritise outcomes for the stakeholders I am responsible for. You must have your solid core principles – once these are set, focus. Don't jump on embracing new vogue issues and the next topic the media says is important. There are always minority issues and groups, but today these can attain a huge voice through the media and social media; that doesn't mean you should abandon serving your core stakeholders or your core values just to accommodate them.

> **RS:** The challenge is the sense that we are 'walking on eggshells – afraid to upset someone or some group every day.' As leaders, we are criticised for what we do and what we don't do. In the US, this has put corporate

communications teams into overdrive with statements [being released] about everything that happens in society.

I was recently criticised for not having timely communication from the organisation to condemn a mass shooting event. Of course, we condemn these things, but here we are, issuing statements several times a month about new developments we only hear about in the news. We are not connected to them, and we have no particular insight or knowledge of the topic – frankly, I'm not sure the media coverage is accurate or complete! I don't think this pressure to say something is healthy; it doesn't make us authentic and risks us saying something inaccurate that could undermine our reputation when we do speak on a topic we actually know something about.

RB: If the woke crowd weren't so loud, we would have the opportunity to do the right thing and be authentic.

(2) The second notion is that while 'responsible leadership' exists as a category, 'leadership' that is not 'responsible' will continue to exist in people's minds. Whereas 'leadership' should be defined, developed and governed with the requirement to be responsible.

KC: Responsible leadership is oxymoronic – how can leadership not be responsible? Leadership is not task- or goal-oriented – it is a holistic concept. Leadership includes aspiration (cognitive), alignment (emotional), acceleration (behavioural), and achievement (ethical).

SG: Previously, it was a lot easier to be a mediocre leader [and] survive for a long time in a business. Now things just ignite, and you have nowhere to hide. There will likely be fewer mediocre leaders in the future because the consequences of mediocrity are severe: the ability to attract investment, talent and to innovate and maintain pace with competitors.

Make Tomorrow Better

The essence of enterprise leadership is being accountable to an array of stakeholders, not too narrowly defined – as the enterprise exists in the context of the broader community, and there is a mutual dependency between the enterprise and the community.

SG: In my view, businesses serve people. A business is a way of organising talents, efforts and resources to create something. It is in the service of people. The original foundational thinking about corporations was that they should benefit people and society. Do you produce goods that genuinely do good? Do you produce services that genuinely serve? Do you think about the impact on future generations and on the environment? Our understanding of what it means to serve society might have changed, but the point of business has always been to serve society. This is what 'lights up the innovation engines'. The purpose of business is actually to support society. It draws in talented people and wins customers who want to buy their products. It's a completely symbiotic relationship.

KC: We cannot give up on ESG (environment sustainability goals). It's hard to do this and make money – it is hard – that's the whole point, leadership is not easy.

TM: I have to communicate to the [company owner] in the language he cares about, but I must be accountable and responsible to a broader set of stakeholders – such as the local community.

ML: [Milton] Friedman would argue that by delivering profit, you are helping society – but this notion is being challenged. Now it is non-discretionary that you have to listen to multiple stakeholders.

JA: Corporations are made up of the best and the brightest in our nation. No institution or governing body can message, innovate and deliver services better than corporations and businesses. I refuse to believe our mandate stops at delivering profits, shareholder return and cash.

Accountability: Measurable and Actionable

I hope this chapter has helped raise awareness and set you thinking about leading responsibly and the essential step, requiring courage to decide who and what you will be accountable to. Moving forward responsibly on the causes and the communities you have prioritised may expose you to criticism for acting irresponsibly towards others. For example, advocates may succeed in driving the government to spend more on healthcare services or to pay healthcare workers more. However, doing so may require the government to spend less on other sectors, such as education. Even if the education funding is not reduced, the fact that the healthcare workers have received a pay rise may increase the sense of entitlement for the workers in education that they, too, should receive similar increases. Leaders are only leaders if they seek to move forward on causes and for stakeholders they have prioritised; leadership is not required if the mission is purely to maintain the status quo. Accountability is more easily tracked and measured than responsibility. 'Did we achieve the outcomes desired by the stakeholders to whom we are accountable?' is a contained question, whereas 'Did we act responsibly?' leaves much space for alternative interpretations dependent on the perspective of the stakeholders and may well vary with time as expectations shift.

To close this discussion, I have included a fascinating and thought-provoking comment from one of the panel members, which sums up the main sentiments of responsible leadership and provides a perspective on the choice of to whom to be accountable.

TM: We choose whether to act responsibly or not. To truly lead, you have to recognise that we are all connected, that you do not live in a silo, you do have responsibility for more than your little world. If you choose not to recognise this, don't be surprised when the fruits are not pleasant when increasingly people don't want to be associated with you and your activities, and when increasingly they pick you up on that and hold you to account. You make a choice in how you show up.

[There is a] Māori concept that you stand with all your forebears to one side and all your descendants on the other – and then the sun shines on you for a short while. When you are in the sun – it is your time to do. You are responsible for continuing the legacy created by all those that came before, and your choices impact all those who will follow.

How would you like to be remembered? How will you be judged for how you have managed what you have inherited? How will we be judged in the future for our contribution? How we will be judged in the future is different to how we have been judged in the past. [There will be] a broader set of criteria.

Life on Earth is short, and ultimately, you would like to think that you have made a difference and that has been a positive difference – and so that requires you to act responsibly. It is a choice. But it should be automatic if you give yourself time to think about it.

Pause, Reflect and Experiment: What Are You Responsible for, to Whom Are You Accountable?

(1) Who are you accountable to?
- Which stakeholders or communities are you sufficiently passionate about that you will/are acting to promote or protect their interests?
  - The more tightly defined the stakeholder groups you are accountable to, the easier it is to know their needs or desires.
- What is the evidence so far, in your life, of your passion in action for these communities?
  - Write down what actions you have taken to date to make a difference.
- Which communities does this mean that you are not prioritising?
  - Are you willing to accept criticism from these groups for not including them/reflecting their wants or needs?

(2) What matters most to the stakeholders you have prioritised and to you?
- Do you have an intimate understanding of the issues these communities are facing?
  - Are you interacting directly with representatives of these communities or relying on intermediaries?
- What are their top 3–5 short, medium, and long-term priorities?
  - Which issues does this mean that you do not need to prioritise?
- What issues will you act on?
  - Are you willing to accept criticism (even from within the communities of stakeholders that you have chosen to be accountable to) for not acting on the other needs or desires?

(3) What actions can you take to pursue these objectives in collaboration with the prioritised stakeholders and others?
- How can you work more closely with members or representatives of the prioritised stakeholder groups?
- Whom will you ask to advise you on your ideas and plans, to provide mentorship or hold you to account?
- What hands-on activities can you do in the short and mid-term?

(4) How do you, or others, assess if you have been accountable or responsible?
- Are you and your efforts known, recognised, and supported by the prioritised stakeholder groups?
- How will you get feedback?
- Who can help you reduce your blind spots and help you avoid unknown errors?
- What are the metrics that you will measure and track?

PART THREE
Ally

Connect and collaborate broadly whilst helping others to thrive. Alliances involve cooperative collaboration between independent entities for mutual benefit, while a hierarchy denotes an authority-based structure where one entity holds a position of higher power or control over another.

Leadership Exists Through Relationships

If 'Leadership is lonely', you're doing it wrong.

TS: You must recognise that you are inspiring and impacting others – so you have a duty to share your thoughts and experiences. Everything you say, each interaction – you should try to add value to others.

In the current environment, where divisions between people, ideologies, beliefs and behaviours are increasingly stark, effective leaders succeed in connecting with and inspiring people who are not like them. In an environment with increasing clamour for individual rights and personal interests, effective leaders demonstrate care for those around them, seeking to support others to thrive. Effective leaders broker trust in a world where the volume of likes of comments, and opinions often substitutes for fact and balanced debate. Enabled by technology, there can now be greater intimacy between leaders and followers at scale. It is in the domain of leading others that there is most evidence of the expanding gulf between truly effective leaders vs the many executives who are in a leadership position but struggle. While effective leaders attract, develop, and retain talent, poor leaders bemoan the talent shortage and the propensity of employees to switch firms.

SB: Care about the people around you – you impact them in every way you interact with them; that is much bigger than the enterprise you work for. Remember and reflect on how you interact with people and make them feel – rather than the projects you have completed or the business results you achieve.

Being responsible for others is at the very core of leadership. Leadership is a relationship between the followers and the leader. Much of this chapter discusses how successful leaders today have a mindset of care and support for others. This authentic care and empathy enable them to effectively connect with and inspire followership from a broad diversity of people, creating conditions where others can flourish while also being true to themselves.

PC: As a leader, you must realise that everyone's view of the world is inherently biased – be big enough to say, 'These guys have a worldview that is legitimate for them – and I need to understand them – and then work out how I adapt: how I interact with them'.

SGJ: I chose to think about building the team for a future without me – rather than me going out in every game and being myself and making the best contribution I could on the court. Instead, my responsibility was to use this tournament, this moment, to build up other players who would step up when I stepped away. Leadership must be selfless. Put your own agenda [and] personal objective aside. I had to realise what a privilege it was to focus on the team and help prepare them for a future without me.

WS: When assessing the emerging leaders in my company, I wonder if they are properly reflecting on the emerging context and the need for change. I'm looking for someone who will inspire trust and has a runway (at least a decade) ahead: they are not just trying to maximise their bonus or optimise what is already here. You must have a sense of responsibility of working for the staff and their families – all their Christmases depend on your leadership.

Chapter 5
Make Connections, Build Relationships

Connect with people NOT like you.

AB: The most successful leaders in the next ten years will be those with exceptional empathy to instil in others a sense of authentic belonging. You have to build 'family'. This may be what many founders in Asia or elsewhere have always done, but if so, we may have forgotten about it. You have to know that you are responsible for the education, health and well-being of the family members of the people who are working for you. As a leader of [a major global corporation], I think this is the biggest change I want to achieve.

To Lead, You Must Make Connections

Leadership involves others, not just ourselves. Yet, a common cry has been that 'leadership is lonely' referring to the isolation of the leader as they alone struggle to carry the burden of responsibility for the collective. In today's dynamic, complex, and fast-changing context, the modern leader should be far from lonely. They cannot put distance between themselves and their would-be followers nor be detached from potential sources of relevant insight. The penetrating vision of social media enables 'followers' to see much more of the real person and amplifies even the small 'signals' to a broader audience. Leaders have always benefited from making emotional connections with their would-be followers; legendary past leaders, such as Churchill, could connect with large populations of dispersed followers by being superb orators and reframing the day's issues to make them resonate with the ordinary citizen. Successful leaders today must bring a similar connection to a more intimate, personal level. Followers today expect their leaders to understand and respond to their needs, concerns and beliefs. If they don't find a resonance with the leadership of their current organisation, it is easy to look elsewhere.

In 2001, Day[26] conceptualised leadership as a social process, while in 2006, Iles and Preece[27] argued that social awareness (empathy, developing others, service orientation, etc.) is critical to leadership development. Bolden and Gosling[28] also argued that leadership has to move to a collective form rather than an individualistic approach. In the social exchange model of leadership, to be accepted and effective, leaders must represent the expectations that their followers have of them.[29] Self-awareness can help leaders understand why they behave in a certain way. Awareness of followers' expectations can help leaders understand why these behaviours may or may not be effective in a particular context. Krauss, Hamid, and Ismail[30] explain that 'Self-aware leaders are sensitive to how their actions affect others and have a greater capacity to adjust to situations'. Thus, the integration of self and social awareness promotes the behavioural adjustments that lead to a more effective interplay between leaders and followers.[31] The social leadership model answers the question 'What makes a leader?' with the reply, 'The followers'!

Be Relatable

Relatability is about showing you're human, giving others an insight into your life with an aspect they can relate to. On the internet, you can find thousands of conversation starters. If you are stuck, scan through some lists and pick out some ideas you would feel comfortable with. Some helpful techniques include:

1. **Say 'Hi' and smile**. We are used to people avoiding eye contact and staring at their phones, so it can be significant when you proactively greet them; it means they have been noticed. Make sure to acknowledge all the people in the room, from the least to the largest! Everyone notices who you speak to and acknowledge.

2. **Ask for an honest opinion**. Ask for their honest opinion on an initiative you have been pursuing or implementing. Ask in an open manner, make it clear that you want to know their thoughts and ideas and that you are open to criticism and constructive feedback.

3. **Bring up a shared interest**. You could start by asking about their experience at the company or why they chose to join it. It is usually safe to talk about family, but not everyone has family members, so be cautious in case that is a sensitive topic; perhaps a relative has just died!

4. **Tell them something about yourself**. By now, probably almost everyone in my company, my clients, many students and coachees past and present know that I love riding horses and motorcycles – I have found that when I share my passions, others tend to reciprocate and tell me what their passions are.

5. **Ask for a helping hand**. When a person helps you, it forms a natural bond; for example, ask how to locate the restroom or connect to the local WIFI, or what local restaurant they enjoy eating at with their family and friends and whether they would recommend it to you; this lowers defences and is immediately personal.

SB: It's critical to connect with the team – they have options to walk away and leave, so you must connect with them. What makes the difference is not the salary – but the people you are working with and the person leading you. You need to reveal things about yourself to encourage others to share – expose your real self – thus, you are a role model for the idea that having more in your life is OK. So, care, yes – but with authenticity. Create a hook for others to engage with you beyond just talking about work. See colleagues as people doing different roles – rather than fixating on the hierarchy. Everyone is a human, with family and life issues – leader or not. They need to see leaders as humans first; I pick the dog poo up like everyone else. ... To break down the barriers that stop the team from connecting with you, you have to give them a hook or two – by sharing things from your life. Being real with people allows them to be real back.

AW: Relatability and vulnerability also determine good leaders. Expressing your natural emotions and weaknesses is hugely relevant to harness relatability. Nothing is worse than a leader being perceived as superior; we are all together, and that's the most important thing to remember from my perspective.

NH: You need to be seen as approachable – Teams (or Zoom) helps with this, as they see me at home, wearing a T-shirt – then the questions come – whereas when I was on stage and doing townhalls, there was far less interactivity.

JH: Today's leader must be extra transparent (showing vulnerability, compassion and care even more than before).

SG: People want to feel more connected to the leader and the cause than before.

Leadership As a Team Sport

Since the beginning of the 21st century, there has been a consistent expansion of the range of issues that concern business leaders and board members, for example, digital transformation, diversity and inclusion, sustainability, geopolitical risk, reputation risk, employer branding, crisis management, etc. Enterprise leaders increasingly must collaborate with others who are experts in these domains rather than themselves, seeking sufficiency in all areas. For much of the first twenty years of the 21st century, the model of the 'T'-shaped leader[32] was promoted. The 'T'-shape comes from the concept that an executive was expected to have grown by building depth of expertise in a domain or area of technical knowledge (perhaps finance), i.e., the stem of the 'T', and then, as they step into roles of general management, they need to extend their understanding to a broader range of areas, i.e., the bar at the top of the 'T'. As the breadth of issues that need to be considered increases and the speed at which new issues emerge accelerates, we see the limitations of the 'T'-shaped leader. Now and increasingly in the future, leaders need to build connections, forming networks and fluid relationships with others with whom they exchange opinions, experiences, insights, concerns, and ideas.

Today's successful leaders are most often found working in collaboration with others, but the notion of the lone heroic leader still lingers in people's imagination. Successful leaders today are adopting arrays of relationships, some within and some external to the organisation. The network of relationships is unique to the individual, and it evolves over time, adapting to the issues being faced. It is impossible for one individual to have sufficient expertise and perspective to manage alone through all the issues and challenges they must navigate the enterprise. There is a need for fluid team-based leadership.

Collective leadership connects people with diverse skills and experiences, often bridging boundaries. There are various labels for types of collective leadership, such as 'shared leadership', 'distributed leadership', 'relational leadership', or 'network leadership', but I prefer the concept of fluid team-based leadership as it retains the expectation that there is a leader of the team, rather than implying a democratic cooperative. The era of the hero-leader who had the ability, experience or bluster to project competence across all the domains pertinent to effectively running the enterprise has passed. The accelerating rate of evolution in multiple domains and directions is driving the continued expansion of the number of specialists required to contribute to the top team; thus, top teams are increasingly complex, and leadership is increasingly a team sport.

RB: If you look at the number of people needed in the board room, it increased explosively from 1980–2010 – and is still increasing. More specialists are required (for DEI, environment, etc.) – the number of perspectives required is higher – and they need to be integrated by the leader.

The age of being good at one thing has come to a close. Employees were less demanding, and social media was less pervasive. Leaders were perhaps (1) good at firm building in relatively stable environments, (2) good at seeing around corners or (3) good at building operational performance. Now a leader needs to be good at managing across these three domains; leadership is evolving to be more of a team sport.

SG: This whole 'CEO is lonely' thing will no longer wash. You are going to have to find ways of sharing the task. You might take customers with you because, by sharing information, you're also sharing responsibility for decision-making. You're listening to other people and [have to be] much more humble. It requires more than one human brain's ability to process what's going on at the right speed and make the right decisions. The key is being humble, integrating and orchestrating conversations, and then getting through each day.

CM: Leaders who lead based on expertise in one [particular] area or experience in the situation will struggle to remain effective.

CU: Collective intelligence; collective leadership needs to contribute to situational awareness – it cannot be one person's responsibility.

Networks and Collaborations

Connecting and collaborating fluidly across boundaries (organisational, cultural, political, etc.) is set to increase. Above I discussed the importance already evident of moving beyond the 'T'-shaped leader to one where collaborating with a network of peers is critical; this capability will grow in importance and be a key differentiator of a leader's effectiveness.

DH: There will be much more collective leadership – team-based leadership. Of course, there will be a focal point/person, but they can't know everything – so a team of specialists must be brought together. Leaders don't have the bandwidth to cover all the topics – that is why they are failing – things come up, and they don't have skills in each area.

TC: The biggest change for leaders in the next ten years will be that they have to accept that they don't understand the content or the roles of the people on their teams. The future general manager needs to understand at a human level how to get the best out of their workforce without necessarily understanding the nuances of what's being done. This becomes more difficult as the technical or technological capabilities become more nuanced. But it's a leadership skill that's absolutely necessary.

Embrace and Accommodate Diversity

There are many arguments in support of embracing greater diversity. These include the ethical and moral arguments of treating everyone equally, the practical argument of ensuring that all pools of talent are considered and embraced and the performance argument that organisations with close attention to the equitable inclusion of diversity perform better than others. A McKinsey & Co. report in 2020[33] noted:

> The growing polarisation between high and low [diversity equity inclusion (DEI) at companies] is reflected in an increased likelihood of a performance penalty. In 2019, fourth-quartile companies for gender diversity on executive teams were 19 per cent more likely than companies in the other three quartiles to underperform on profitability – up from 15 per cent in 2017 and 9 per cent in 2015. At companies in the fourth quartile for both gender and ethnic diversity, the penalty was even steeper in 2019: they were 27 per cent more likely to underperform on profitability than all other companies.

DEI is a key issue for many leaders committed to equity and inclusion for everyone while embracing talent from all communities.

AW: Respect individuality and embrace it. The world and business are made up of people. If people cannot be true to themselves and you cannot be true as a leader, then you cannot truly sustain your position.

MH: DEI is important – not rainbow washing: setting conditions that mean teams have the context to thrive. [We need] real equality and inclusion, not just a 'ticket' to be included. I don't think we have this right yet. We include folks not on merit. We don't create the environment for DEI folks to succeed.

BL: Soft skills in managing diverse teams and people will become more important as each generation of employees grows from the Internet Age to the Information Age, then to the Metaverse Age.

JH: There is so much richness in diversity of point of view, which I will again embrace in my new role with six countries with strong cultures and traditions.

Leaders are aware that the pursuit of quotas and target ratios for representation can be impractical or counterproductive; diversity goals need to reflect the population pools specifically relevant to their context.

KH: We have mainly white and middle-class employees because few ethnically diverse folks seem to want to work in the environmental sector. How does this get changed – or even should it be – i.e., should we find ways of going into the ethnic groups and telling them/encouraging them to become more caring about the environment or working for the environment? Sure, that would help our ability to employ more folks from these communities – but by doing that – aren't we trying to make them become more like us? If we respected their diversity – why would we try to get them to change their preferences for where they want to work?

SB: [When it comes to] DEI – you need to see the context that you are in. You can't be disrespectful of the minority communities by telling them that they should work for you/your sector just so that you can hit your diversity quotas. This area [of Scotland] has a very small ethnic population; to reach the expected quotas set by our headquarters, we would have to import people.

SB2:   There is too much political correctness and woke-ism. Leaders must adapt to this reality where the form may be more important than the substance. In our firm, we have quotas for age, religion, gender, and ethnicity; this is more important than the quality of each candidate. Companies are relying too much on quantitative assessments (we had to write a 4-page justification to hire an intern to comply with the process for hiring)

Managing for DEI can be highly complex, as illustrated by the story of a digital marketing executive, 'Poon', from Thailand, who worked for a leading global FMCG corporation.

Poon had progressed rapidly through various roles after joining the company from university in Bangkok, Thailand. At 29, she led the national digital marketing team and regularly collaborated with colleagues regionally and sometimes on global projects. Although Poon spoke English very well, she was conscious that her voice and ideas were often not heard in the regional and global teams; perhaps she didn't communicate forcefully enough, but her voice was a part of her identity.

That year, she was offered a promotion and invited to join the Global High-Potential Talent programme, a career, training, and experience accelerator for individuals destined for regional or even global roles. After careful consideration, Poon refused, much to the surprise of HR and the regional Marketing Director, who had endorsed Poon's promotion and expected to welcome Poon to the regional team based in Singapore. Her reasons for rejecting the offer emerged through a series of informal discussions. She lived in a multi-generational family home in a suburb of Bangkok with a grandparent, parents, sisters, nieces and nephews. Her father had worked his entire career at the Thai subsidiary of a US auto parts manufacturer, mainly as a mid-level manager. 2009 he was made redundant after the corporation was restructured following the 2008 financial crisis. In accordance with their practices for local workers, there was only a minimal severance package, which left the family with debt on the house. Poon and her sister (who worked for a local telecom operator) financially supported the family. The increased pay that Poon would receive with the now-offered promotion would be welcomed by the family (and Poon). However, the move to Singapore would mean that she was not at home to support her relatives and was putting trust, for her future, in a foreign company, as her father had once done. Becoming a member of the Global High-Potential Talent programme would possibly require her to move farther away, even out of the region; this would mean a greater distance from her family and greater dependence on the corporation. At 29, Poon was also thinking about relationships and perhaps a few years away from starting a family of her own, which she felt would be highly unlikely were she to move away. She was aware that it was possible she would be in a senior executive role when she reached 40 years old. Still, it would come at the cost of being single and alone in a remote country while missing the family's milestones and always feeling concerned about whether the corporation would restructure or outsource her role. This vision was not only unattractive; it was terrifying. Poon also wondered why, as she was running digital marketing campaigns, it was even necessary for her to move away from Thailand; surely everything could be conducted virtually. There were subsequent discussions between Poon, the Regional Marketing Director, and the HR team, but global policies could only be stretched so far. She ended up leaving the multinational and joining a team at the telecoms operator where her sister worked. If she had needed it, this was a further reminder that career resilience comes from your own network of relationships, not loyalty to a foreign corporation.

Poon's story illustrates some of the difficulties firms face in pursuing DEI. There may be a genuine intention to embrace diversity (for example, anyone from anywhere can be invited into the Global High-Potential Talent pool); however, the policies were conceived from a particular cultural perspective (where it is considered attractive to have international assignments, and where adult children are not expected to take on responsibility for the wider family). Their universal application, intended to ensure equal opportunities and avoid biases, in practice, mitigates against inclusion. The regional HR lead of the corporation where Poon had worked commented, 'It's not that we don't want people of all nationalities and cultures to have equal opportunities; we strenuously do want that. We expect people from every country, culture, and creed to behave the same way so that our policies and practices can accommodate them!'

Foster the Sense of Belonging: Community

In the context of the new normal, with high instability and rapid change, an organisation's culture has heightened importance. People want to feel they belong, are respected and cared for, and can thrive in the environment. There is a significantly decreased tolerance of environments where individuals cannot be true to who and how they are. I recently visited the headquarters of two global corporations, both located in the same city in the USA. One was resident in a new suite of modern offices, which they had curated carefully to be employee-centric, providing an extensive array of services on-site, including day-care, feeding rooms, nap rooms, massage, hairdressing, pet care, gym, a resident barista and an extensive array of alternative menu options. The other was rather tired looking, not having been renovated for at least 15 years. It had large open-plan areas and banks of console cubicles, and I spotted quite a few stained carpet squares with corners that rounded upwards. However, this was the office that was humming with people and conversations, while the employee-centric designed office was largely deserted. The CEO with the tired-looking office explained that they had decided to invest in building community rather than facilities. Employees were empowered to find and pursue activities related to causes, clubs and activities that mattered to them. So long as ten or more staff were involved, the company would support them.

AJ: Community is so important – so everyone knows where they fit, are valued, and have a place and a high sense of belonging. People do not have to change themselves to fit in a certain environment – and feel they belong, whoever they are. Colour, race or creed should not matter. The culture as it is lived is the last 0.5% of performance that makes the difference – everything we do now is about community, culture and values; what we do comes second to that.

OL: The culture of community where people feel belonging; mutual support, where they can lean on each other; sufficient connection between colleagues: this brings people into the workplace, not the quality of the chairs and the features you put on for people.

Develop and Use Emotional Intelligence

Far from leading a homogenous workforce of 'people like me', leaders today need to be able to connect with, motivate and inspire a broad diversity of individuals. Often the leader may be in a minority group. Increasingly, leaders speak about the significance of differences between the generations comprising the workforce. As the founder and CEO of a green-tech business that recently celebrated its 35th anniversary noted:

WS: The majority of my staff are now either Gen Z or X. Most of them, I am sure, don't regard me as a role model; they don't want to be like me. It's because of my choices regarding my attitude to work and the lack of boundaries between my personal and work life. I can't lead them by saying, 'This is how I am; follow me'. I have to understand what motivates and causes them to worry and stress. It's humbling. I sometimes wonder how I dragged us through the first 20 years, just charging ahead and expecting followership.

TS: Leaders need to be able to engage with those unlike them – and to understand them.

SG: Compassion is really important now. Compassion has come back really strongly. It's not about having a position and people following you mindlessly. It's rawer now; there must be an emotional connection.

TC: There is such a vast number of personal aspects that impact somebody's ability to do their job. For example, [consider] an individual who won't comply and is very negative – well, a new manager doesn't know how to deal with that because they don't understand how different external factors can impact somebody's productivity. That might be their mental health, family situation, historical experience of a particular situation, or a particular job they've undertaken. The new manager has to be able to shift away from work-based solutions to understanding more about the person, almost in a psychological manner; new managers/new leaders need to understand the triggers, to understand the things that motivate and derail – particularly in mental health.

RC: Across generations, this is even more important. Connections need to be built and understanding of one another – then get the alignment, find personal things to be aligned on – and build from that.

Overwhelmingly, leaders speak about the need to develop and exercise genuine empathy towards others: the ability to 'see it as they see it' and 'feel it as they feel it'. Empathic leadership adopts the mindset that we are all connected, and that leadership is a social activity involving interactions and co-dependency rather than transactions. Empathy is the ability to sense the other person's emotions from their perspective and respond appropriately without losing sight of one's perspective, responsibilities, and objectives. Empathetic leaders seek ways to respond to followers' motivations and constraints, finding ways to accommodate individual circumstances within transparent guidelines and constraints.

One of the most effective ways to develop an understanding of others is to adopt a deliberate 'pause' in a discussion. In that pause, seek only to understand the other person. Firstly, determine their emotion and feeling rather than seeking to tease out the logic of their thinking. Someone's feelings and emotions, as they are experiencing them, are their reality at that time. Once their feelings are discussable, seek to understand why they are feeling that way, who the participants are and what have been the actions that have created the situation that has led to their emotions; it will rarely be one person or one action. The third step is to enquire what, if anything, the individual thinks you can do to improve their situation. What you decide to do, if anything, is up to you. Any action should be considered for your objectives and responsibilities, made with fairness towards others and with transparency. Whether and however you act, the individual will still appreciate that you have asked – and listened. The good news is that empathy can be developed and that it can be infectious. As the leader, how you demonstrate empathy will influence those in your team to practice empathy in their teams.

TB: Ten to 15 years ago, I would have been more single-mindedly focused on the commercials, whereas now I recognise that my teams are far more productive when they are happy, they are comfortable with their work, and they have a clear understanding of what we are trying to achieve together and how that links to the success of the customers. A recent example is when one of my Ops managers needed time to care for an elderly relative but felt conflicted that they couldn't take time out of the day to attend a hospital appointment. They were shocked when I said to take whatever time they needed. We are not in an industry that is [a matter of] life and death; what was more important right at that moment was that the family member needed their support. Some work could wait, and I pushed out the deadlines so that other work could be reallocated around them. The immediate response was gratitude, and they dealt with their family issue. The longer-term impact is that this Ops manager now takes that same approach with family issues that she's faced, with her much broader team of around 60-line reports, coordinated through four or five team managers. The trickle-down of that approach to doing the right thing for individuals has decreased the amount of sickness we have as a team, increased productivity and reduced our attrition.

TC: Leaders need to be empathetic: I was in a meeting this week when a senior manager was talking quite openly about their very expensive new car ... and I was thinking, 'That's just not the right thing to be doing'; that manager didn't display any empathy with people in the audience who might have been struggling to make ends meet or to rearrange their budgets.

Empathic behaviour enables forming emotional bonds with the leader, which enhances a sense of belonging and a feeling of interconnectedness and strengthens team identity.[34] Listening and empathy are critical for building trust in a team[35] and supporting team performance.[36] Empathy makes resonance possible, whereas the lack of it creates dissonance.[37]

The tasks within job scopes and scheduling when and where the work should be conducted can evolve as a result of listening empathetically to employees. A CIPD[38] report discusses the case of City Sightseeing in Glasgow. The company asks employees how many hours they would like to work and then seeks to adjust their work schedules. The practice is equitably applied to all employees so that they can accommodate and reflect the particular concerns of different groups of employees, for example, older employees seeking to work fewer hours, or those with caring responsibilities for young or old relatives, or students who are fitting work around their studies.

Empathy is rarely the characteristic people rank most highly as essential for leadership. Indeed, Holt and Marques[39] reported that business school students initially place empathy lowest on a list of skills needed for leadership. However, when the students have participated in activities and exercises that raise their awareness of empathy, they realise its greater importance.

Develop and Use a Repertoire of Styles

A high level of empathy assists the leader in understanding the individuals that they are leading. As every individual is different, the leader must have a range of styles to be effective with each person. High empathy but a 'one-size-fits-all' single leadership style will not be effective. However, a popular perspective on leadership is that each leader has a particular dominant style, which leads to the notion that you want to have the right leader at the right time. For example, a visionary, highly energised entrepreneur may be great at the start-up stage but not suited to growing the enterprise to having 1,000 employees. A leader required to drive through a turnaround amid a crisis may not be the leader required to build a robust innovation pipeline for the long-term success of the enterprise, etc. In business today, turbulence is the new normal; growth, maturity and disruption may coexist. Successful leaders today must have a portfolio of leadership styles, adapting appropriately to the different audiences and issues they face while still being true to themselves. Leadership has changed.[40]

RS: Society is sometimes enamoured with 'hero leaders' who are provocative, charismatic, and bold (Welch, Musk, Ma, Jobs, Bezos etc.), yet we see little evidence that this persona is effective in most contexts. The right leader for the future might be more boring than people might like or expect.

Daniel Goleman suggests that 'each [leadership] style springs from different components of emotional intelligence.' He identifies six styles: coercive and authoritative; affiliative; democratic; pacesetting; and coaching.[41] He compares these styles to golf clubs. Using only one club for a full round of golf would be highly unusual. Instead, according to Goleman, leaders with the best results do not rely on only one leadership style; they use most of them each week – seamlessly and in different ways – depending on the situation. Research shows that the leader's style affects job satisfaction, motivation, and team performance and, therefore, the leader's effectiveness.[42] I wouldn't limit the set of possible styles to six; each leader must evolve their authentic repertoire. However, I agree with the 'golf club' analogy; to be effective, leaders need to be proficient in using multiple different 'clubs' (styles) and know when to use each.

PC: Those leaders who say 'those darn Gen Z types' are the very leaders who need to become more adaptive; they need to be more empathetic and learn to understand them. Talent will go where the better, more adaptable leaders are, the companies where they will thrive. It's the end of mediocre leadership – i.e., those with one style. Leaders need to be adaptive. Look at where you are and how you are trying to lead – do you always bring one style, or are you adaptable?

TC: The 'Steve Jobs' strong leader model would be less likely to be as effective if he tried to do the same thing today. You need to be a 'situational' leader, e.g., asking someone confident and experienced and skilled to do something (maybe delegate and ask them to get on with it) is very different to the way you would ask someone new or less confident (which might be much more [about] coaching and encouragement and giving them very specific details – you build them up by demonstrating how they should do it).

Bill George's model of authentic leadership,[43] anticipates that leaders pursue purpose and prioritise values and self-discipline while leading with the heart. It is not inauthentic to adapt leadership styles; it is smart and strategic. Leaders must adapt their styles to changing contexts to lead effectively today and in the future.[44]

MH: Leaders need to spend a lot of time with people and try to understand where they're coming from – and I think that may change their perspective. I don't think people go from authentic to inauthentic when they change. People change all the time; it's called learning.

Pause, Reflect and Experiment: Make Connections, Build Relationships

(1) In your enterprise and beyond, who do you more readily connect with, and who are you less connected to?
  • What patterns do you notice as you reflect on these groups of people?
    – Do you have biases? Conscious or not?
  • Why do you have an inner circle and others?
    – How do people become a part of your inner circle – and how do they leave (or do they?)

(2) Connect with others, especially those NOT like you and NOT in your inner circle.
- Decide who you need to better connect with.
- How are you going to build connections with them?
- What aspects of your persona can you reveal or deploy to provide a bridge through which to build personal connections with individuals across the enterprise?
- Make it a rule that you will always, in every situation, seek to make a connection with someone new. Ensure that you are relatable.

(3) Seek to understand: experiment with the 'deliberate pause' technique described in this chapter. When engaged in an animated discussion with someone, make a deliberate pause, switching your focus to understanding the other person starting with their emotion, then once able to discuss their feelings, seek to understand why they are feeling that way and what, if anything, they think you might be able to do to improve the situation. Remember that what you decide to do – if anything – is up to you.

(4) Build empathy into the culture of the enterprise: discuss the importance of empathy and what good practice might look like in your organisation or team. Techniques that you might role model and encourage people to adopt could include the following:
- *Walk a mile in their shoes*. Find ways to directly experience the work and context of the other person or team members. For example: (1) shadowing – whereby you follow them through their day, living it alongside them; (2) swapping places – whereby you undertake the role of the other person for a day or so; or (3) undercover boss – be placed into a team or role where they do not recognise you as a leader of the organisation.
- *Role-playing*. Individuals are assigned to characters and asked to ad-lib, unscripted, through prescribed situations. They may be provided with a briefing note on the character they take on or take on the role of a person known to them in the organisation. There follows a discussion between the group members about what they know or believe about that character (with the key points being captured on a whiteboard).

- *Conducting meetings more empathetically:* adopt a room layout or seating format where everyone is equal (as in King Arthur's Round Table!) Start with a centring exercise so everyone is focused on this meeting and aware of everyone's time and potential contribution. Then, discussing each topic, ensure that concerns, hopes, challenges and opportunities are always aired. Ensure that each person speaking is accorded the same attentive listening and honest questioning.

(5) Learn to adapt your style of leading and interacting. Be more effective in more situations by adapting to the dynamics and individuals involved.
  - Understand different leadership styles and raise your ability to switch between styles depending on the situation.
  - Raise your ability to read the room/situation.
  - Match your message to the moment.
  - Increase your capacity for social judgement.

Chapter 6
Collaborate: Alliances and Teams

Build alliances not hierarchies: Roles are temporary,
relationships fluid, memories are forever.

Alliances

Long before the 'Great Resignation' the average tenure in a position had been steadily decreasing; it is now considered the exception to remain in position beyond 3 years. A member of your team today may tomorrow be your customer, competitor, representing a shareholder, influencing regulation, supplying you with new technology solutions and systems or a vocal critic or supporter on social media. Even when you are working together you are probably unaware of much of their activities, their life, beliefs, and passions outside the context of your work. Sooner or later, you will be in different contexts, different roles, however, how they remember their time with you, the impact, positive or negative, that you have had on them will endure. As such, I believe that we should adopt the mindset of building alliances that will endure beyond the current roles, not being blinkered by today's hierarchy relationship.

SB: We are all equal, but we are each playing different roles at this point in time, in this particular setting.

"Allyship is a personal dedication to look outside yourself and do for others in ways that you would have them do unto you."

Earl Newsome, Chief Information Officer at Cummins.[45]

When asked what is the measure of team performance, most people initially make reference to the achievement of the anticipated outcomes, however, increasingly we recognise that great team performance is the product of great experiences for the team members. As Bill Walsh, the legendary manager of the San Francisco 49ers American Football team noted in his book *The Score Takes Care of Itself*.[46] 'Culture,' he says, 'precedes positive results', which he follows up with 'You need to stretch people to help them achieve their full potential [...] the most powerful way to do this is by having the courage to say, "I believe in you." These four words constitute the most inspirational message a leader can convey.' I believe that the more we focus on the experience of colleagues, building them up and supporting them to be the best that they can be, the better the outcomes for the collective and the individual. We may only be together for a short time, but the positive experiences of our time together will be carried inside us for our lifetimes and will 'ripple out' to positively impact others.

Teams

As individuals move between roles and organisations, it is helpful to think of them coming together in fluid teams whether within or across departments, whether a project or a standing team, whether all members are from one or several enterprises. Leaders should have the mindset and adopt the behaviours and practices for effective teaming in all situations. Team performance is so important that it cannot be left to chance as we address an increasingly broad array of initiatives.[47] The way a team comes together, the way the individuals of a team interact with each other, and the way they behave and coordinate with stakeholders outside the team should be explicit, a codified set of behaviours and expectations. There should be an explicit doctrine of teaming matched to the specific enterprise.

RS: Now, more than ever, it is a team sport. Success is determined by forming and leading good teams.

IS: Get the most out of your team, developing people or replacing them – with due process and care – but focus on the team's performance – with the right behaviours (including the Argyris stuff [this refers to Chris Argyris, who we will discuss later]). Make sure you are having evidence-based discussions.

BJ: The most important thing you have is the team's human capital – do you have the right people on your team? What can you do to improve this? Fix it fast. The best way to advance and have the most impact is to have the best team working for you.

PC: Build teams with agility.

SGJ: Leadership is about teamwork; it's not a static position; it's forever evolving. [You need the] mindset that leadership is moving, changing – not static. The leader must think that they are always evolving – and this involves others – as the leadership team morphs.

NH: Build really strong, diverse teams around you. They share the vision and have the capability to make the decisions daily – [the need to be able to] course-correct without needing too much support and direction from me; [this involves a] sense of conviction and courage to move forward.

RP: Those leaders that cut through are the ones who unite their team around a sense of positive purpose, show a genuine concern for others and maintain a consistently fair and open approach in both the good and bad times. They can manage their own stress without passing it on directly to their teams, and they are able to change gears where necessary so that everyone knows when it's time to push.

Doctrine of Teaming

The life stages of teams coined by Tuckman in 1965[48] (Forming-Storming-Norming-Performing and then Dissolving) remains relevant today. It is particularly useful in providing a common language for team members to discuss what they are each experiencing and where (at which stage) they think they are as individuals and collectively. In the overview of the Tuckman stages of the life of a team below, I have embedded the six key questions of the doctrine of teaming that should be discussed and agreed upon by team members if the team is to be high-performing. It is important to acknowledge that there is rarely a linear process from one stage to the next; instead, stages need to be revisited as the team adapts to changes in context, objectives, timelines or other factors and as members leave and join in mid-flow.

In the Forming stage, individuals are still determining the team's purpose, how they fit in, and whether they'll work well with one another. They may be anxious, curious, or excited to get going. However, they feel, they'll be looking to the team leader for direction. Key questions to discuss and achieve alignment on are:

1. **What exactly is the mandate of this team**; why is this mandate important for the wider organisation, and how is it different from every other team or part of the organisation? What is this team accountable for, and what is outside of its remit? Is the mandate of this team unique and important, or is it overlapping with the mandate of other teams? In 'Leading Teams,'[49] Richard Hackman points out the need to 'establish a compelling direction for the team', which requires getting the balance between giving teams too much direction and giving them too little (e.g., a vague description of the team's purposes and leaving it to the team to 'work out the details').

2. **What kind of team are we**; Is this a working team, a coordinating team or for governing etc.? What is the limit of what this team is responsible for doing, where do others take over, who are they, and what is the interface with them? Setting a good direction for a team means being <u>authoritative</u> and insistent about desired end states but equally insistent about not specifying how the team should achieve those end states, allow the team to decide.

3. **Who should be in the core team** to enable the team to fulfil its duties? Which skills and what level of seniority is required to enable it to function well? What size should the team be to be effective and efficient? The principle should be that everyone on the team is contributing equally. The ideal team size is four to six people, emphasising heterogeneity. Teams of three often fall into routines dominated by personality and are unlikely to have the breadth of skills and insights required for the most complex issues. In teams with above six members, it is common to see some individuals being 'passengers' drawn along by the process rather than having an equal contribution. Guests (perhaps expert voices) may be invited into the team discussions if required rather than being included in the team membership.
   - During the Forming stage, team members should share personal goals and constraints that will be relevant for this period of being together in the team.

In the Storming stage, friction can arise between team members or against the boundaries within which they are supposed to operate – or even the mission and mandate. During this period, it is essential to establish what Google calls 'Psychological Safety' – i.e., team members respect and trust one another enough to freely express relevant thoughts, feelings, successes, mistakes and problems. Prof. Amy Edmondson of Harvard Business School highlights four actions that the leader needs to take to help to build up psychological safety:

- **Set the Stage:** Its complex, Its Important, Uncertainty, Complexity, No-one knows, I don't know; we need everyone's ideas and thoughts. Provide the rationale for why everyone's voice is needed.

- **Proactively Invite the Voice of Others:** Ask individuals what they see and think. Ask directly to individuals; ask open-ended questions.

- **Demonstrate Listening and Curiosity**: Seek to understand what they are saying and how they are thinking. What does that mean? What are the potential implications? Ask who else can build on that comment.

- **Don't Shoot the Messenger**: Respond in a forward-looking appreciative manner. Do not act defensively. Do not suggest that was a good (or bad) suggestion.

In the Norming stage, people start to resolve their differences, appreciate one another's strengths, and respect the leader's authority. A stronger commitment to the team's goals emerges, and momentum builds. Two key Teaming Doctrine questions are:

4. **What behaviours are expected from everyone in the team?** Everyone should be held accountable by everyone else in the team for behaving in the manner that has been agreed. Everyone should contribute to the team's success in approximately equal proportions.
   - Google's research into what makes for good team performance (Project Aristotle)[50] identified the following norms:
     - Everyone on the team talks and listens in roughly equal measure, keeping contributions short.
     - Members face one another, and their conversations and gestures are energetic.
     - Members connect directly with one another, not just with the team leader.
     - Members carry on back-channel or side conversations within the team.
     - Members periodically break, explore outside the team, and bring back new information and insight.

In the Performing stage, the team is in-the-flow and performing well. The team will likely achieve its goals with hard work and good processes. Members may take on roles and responsibilities more fluidly to support one another. Differences between members broaden and strengthen the capabilities and performance of the team.

- Members simultaneously hold each other to account by challenging and questioning one another while reinforcing the messages and actions of support to one another (as indicated in Figure 6.1).

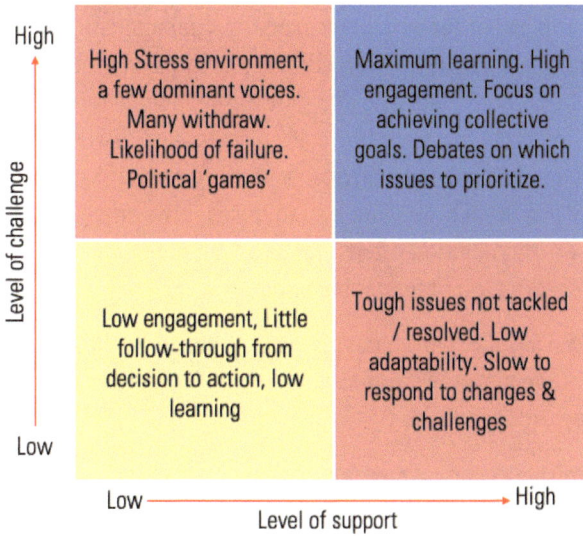

Figure 6.1

- Monitor the behaviours of all team members and interpersonal dynamics. Address all areas of concern immediately and set and hold high standards for everyone on the team, including:
  - Each individual's commitment to this team; are they taking personal responsibility for collective performance?
  - Are they participating actively in decision-making processes?
  - How are they representing this team to the wider organisation?
  - Are they reinforcing or undermining Psychological Safety,
  - Are they building up trust and affinity between themselves and other team members?
  - Are team members able and comfortable to switch between different roles/styles to improve the dynamics of discussions and the team's functioning, or do they stick with one voice, whether constructive or not?

5. **How does this team interface and align with other parts of the organisation?** Are the members of this team in this 'tribe' (taking on the primary identity of this team), or are they representatives of other parts of the organisation (other tribes)? What is the dependence or independence of this team from the actions, resources or priorities of the other parts of the organisation? How do we ensure appropriate transparency and manage all dependencies?

6. **How does this team learn and improve?** A characteristic of high-performing teams is the quality of the learning that is taking place. How do team members or stakeholders share feedback, and how does the team renew itself if required? I recommend that teams also have collective learning discussions, both periodic and event based. They might involve post-mortem discussions to explore what worked well and what didn't, but also to uncover the emotions and perceptions of each team member, as often these can be overshadowed by the general belief and observation of team processes.

AW: Get to know your teammates as well as you can; that doesn't mean best friends. It means knowing their tendencies, what makes them tick, and how best to provide feedback.

IS: Giving and receiving proper feedback without getting defensive [is crucial]. Analyse the culture [in terms of] what they say and do.

In the Dissolving stage, teams disband, and projects end. Members who have developed close working relationships with colleagues may find this stage difficult.

- A discipline should be adopted whereby, whenever a team disbands, or individuals rotate out, there is a debrief of what has worked well and what can be improved. Team members and the doctrine of teaming for the organisation should always be improving.

Quickly establishing effective teams is particularly important in dynamic contexts (which are increasingly the norm) where the reliance on smoothly forming and disbanding teams can be a source of competitive advantage. As each team comes together, there should be an onboarding which aligns all the members – with each understanding the mandate, behavioural norms, learning mechanisms and responsibilities of being a member of this team.

Win With Identity, Anchored on Purpose

Much of my work involves supporting 'strong' teams to be 'exceptional', whether sports or senior executive teams. These are teams where individual members are regarded as being at or near the 'top of their game'. What differentiates the exceptional vs the good teams is the level of personal responsibility for collective performance – yes, personal responsibility and effort!

It has been said that a high-performing team is like a 'well-oiled machine'; I disagree. A well-oiled machine is one where the component parts, the team members, are all strong, well-designed for their role and fit together. The movements of such a team are well-practised, and the operations are smooth, so execution is near flawless; the team responds to the direction of the coach (leader). This can be a good team, a strong team – they might expect to be at the top of their league, but it takes that extra 'half a per cent' to be exceptional, the winning team.

The intertwining of self with collective identity leads to greater adaptability in support of others while also striving to excel in one's primary role. Imagine an outstanding striker in a soccer team who is seemingly always able to be in the right place at the right time and make incredible shots on target – and yet is also willing to drop back and fill other gaps that emerge through the game's flow. Thus he/she maintains an incredible work rate and gives confidence to teammates to push on further while frustrating the opposition. In contrast, highly skilled team members often define themselves through their role and how well they perform that role rather than the collective performance.

In an exceptional team, each player (member), while striving to be the best they can be for the position they hold, identifies their personal success and own reputation through the success and reputation of the team, not a financial bonus or reward, nor the expectation of increasing their visibility for new job opportunities. Instead, there is a strong sense of purpose, something important that everyone is strongly committed to achieving, a commonly-shared vision – that can only be achieved together. These team members imagine the story they will tell their grandchildren of having played their part in achieving that vision. ''Yes, I was in the team that won the [World/League] Cup' ... or 'Yes, I was one of the original team members that grew company X, pioneering the industry that is now synonymous with this city'.

RC: Stand for things together, emotionally invested in it together (e.g., a private, group goal beyond the corporate goal). Make sure the team is more than transactional – it's a community of purpose and belonging.

MH: Help people see themselves in the greater picture, striving to achieve the purpose that the organisation has adopted. Put them in that picture.

AJ: The lines between work and your life are blurred now. You can't separate it. People need to feel a purpose connects them, and the person who is leading that is genuine and authentic. Be clear on where you want to take people and how you want to make the journey, not just the result.

Rather than the discipline of the 'well-oiled machine', I prefer to use the analogy of the symphony orchestra. The personality of each musician adds nuances to how the music they produce sounds; they are all individuals with different shapes, sizes, pieces of training, backgrounds and personalities. While all are playing the same concert piece, the conductor blends everyone's efforts, giving the nod and eye contact with each musician as required, ensuring they are seen and heard for what they are doing. While every concert will be different, the quality of the performances can always be excellent if they play in harmony.

AJ: Winning is not enough any longer: people used to accept negative behaviours in the pursuit of the goal of winning. They want to feel valued, appreciated, respected, nurtured – just people, more than athletes. The leader needs to look after this process – this will attract the best talent aligned with these values – and then success will come.

PC: Leadership – focus on the process, not the outcome; results will come. Like that great book, *The Score Takes Care of Itself*.[51] Get the foundations right.

Teams Are Not Democracies

Embracing diversity in the skills and perspectives that individuals bring to the team is widely recognised as positive, helping to address the breadth of issues and factors required to pursue the enterprise's mission. Equally, there must be good processes and practices so that, while everyone contributes, the team remains focused and productive. Balancing these two priorities means it is rarely appropriate to regard the team as a democracy, where consensus is always necessary. Diversity of contribution, constructive debate, and decision alignment are more important than apparent consensus. Leaders must remain responsible and accountable for timely decision-making. Inclusion in the team is not the same as the team being a democracy.

TM: Engage and learn from them collectively and individually, but ultimately [there] needs to be a decision, direction, and action. Listen to and engage with the team – and then act. This is not delegation; you do not want [to prioritise] consensus. I don't believe this is possible or right – as ultimately, you have to make the decision. There are things that I, as a leader, am accountable for. People want vision, action and leadership – but it's not just telling people; you listen to what they say, then decide whether, how, and when to act.

CU: In such a complex and dynamic world, where the rules are always changing, there is diminishing utility in an autocratic leader. But I don't see this model going away in a hurry. However, there has been a shift toward having a 'democratic' leader, which has gone too far; being so sensitive to the needs of the people means that they have forgotten how to be directive and assertive. Assertiveness is an essential ingredient, whereas it is somehow seen as outdated. I've seen more damage done by leaders failing to be assertive at the right time and failing to lead. Collective leadership has led to the demise of assertiveness [which can create] delays, [during which] much damage can be done to the organisation and the team morale.

RC: Alignment is not the same as agreement – alignment is being dedicated to getting it done and being open about difficulties. In South America, we would make a Friday lunch once a month and stay all afternoon – have drinks and chat about everything.

AI: Collaborate with your team; [make an] inclusive environment so they can all contribute. But you are not looking for compromises between opinions – you need to chart the path of choice. Be a leader, not a politician.

NH: [You need a] sense of conviction and courage to move forward through cabinet leadership. You can have a debate in the room, debate and challenge – with high support and alignment on the goals and vision. [But they must be] united on the message and actions when they walk out of the room. There must be a high level of trust in the senior leader.

SG: You are leaving yourself quite vulnerable now – as you leave it out on the table, share your concerns, and ask for others' inputs and insights. But [you don't want] 'too many cooks in the kitchen'; you must still make decisions and drive forward – that is why you, the leader, are there.

Jeff Bezos and Larry Page have been outspoken against the pursuit of consensus in decision-making. Consensus nearly always slows decisions and often doesn't lead to a good or better one, as the group and interpersonal dynamics may be unconstructive. The person with the most energy may continue to argue their case while everyone else is exhausted and needs to get on with other tasks – resulting in a false consensus. Larry Page established his formula for group decision-making at Google to include the following criteria: (1) Every meeting must have <u>one clear decision-maker.</u> If there's no decision-maker — or no decision to be made — the meeting shouldn't happen. (2) No more than ten people should attend. (3) Every person should give input; otherwise, they shouldn't be there. (4) No decision should ever wait for a meeting. If a meeting absolutely has to happen before a decision can be made, then the meeting should be scheduled immediately.

As a part of Sir Alex Ferguson's 'Ferguson Formula' for successful teams, Rule 4 (of 10) is 'never, ever cede control'. He explained that, as the leader, 'You can't ever lose control [...] if any players want to take me on, to challenge my authority and control, I deal with them.'[52] As Sir Alex describes it, 'I tended to act quickly when I saw a player become a negative influence. Some might say I acted impulsively, but I think it was critical that I made up my mind quickly. Why should I have gone to bed with doubts? I would wake up the next day and take the necessary steps to maintain discipline. It's important to have confidence in yourself to make a decision and to move on once you have. It's not about looking for adversity or opportunities to prove power; it's about having control and being [decisive] when issues arise.'

Decision-Making in Teams

The process for taking a decision should reflect the decision to be made and the context in which it is being made. Jeff Bezos, while pressing for 'high-velocity decision making', notes that most decisions are reversible, so he encourages taking them quickly and moving on. Those that are truly non-reversible will thus merit more complex processes. Some techniques that can help ensure inclusiveness, which may foster, yet do not depend upon, achieving consensus, include:

1. Defining the problem (or dilemma) and inviting open debate rather than presenting potential solutions to be discussed, refined, and endorsed.
   - Require the group to put forward three or four plausible alternative solutions.
   - Expect and manage disagreement, make sure that the disagreement does not become personal and that differences do not continue outside the meeting room.
   - Ensure that there is a safe space, with high psychological safety, for members to speak up, contribute and challenge one another.

2. Diverge and converge. First, diverge. Everyone contributes ideas and insights that enrich the overall understanding of the issue. Then converge on the two most important while also integrating insights.
   - Double diverge-converge from the two ideas emerging from the first pass, then diverge again, e.g., adding options or alternative refinements to each one. Then converge again to the two most suitable. Everyone should note the benefits and challenges of each of the remaining options to inform further taking the eventual decision.
     - The advantages of this process are reduced individual ownership and advocacy of the final solutions that emerge – and greater collective awareness of the constraints.

3. Red team: For any decision to be taken, someone (or a team) who is credible is tasked with arguing against it. Avoid frequently giving this task to the most junior person, as this can discredit the process and alienate the individual.

4. The negative proposition: The opposite of the proposed solution is formulated and described. The group then discusses why that opposite solution is or is not feasible.

5. The Delphi technique: This process can consume significant time and is often used to arrive at, or nearly at, a consensus on a decision in a complex or ambiguous situation. A simpler version of this method is to collect opinions independently and then consider, combine and distil these towards a solution/recommendation.
   - Each person responds independently to the problem statement or question. The key is to collect the inputs and insights independently to reduce the opportunity for biases about what has been said based on who is saying it.
   - The responses are aggregated and integrated by a moderator who then shares their output with the team members again, with no reference to who has said what.
   - They then debate the different opinions – and once more submit their individual responses, which will usually have changed from the first round due to the debate and hearing the shared insights. These are then integrated again by the moderator.
   - The process continues as above until there are two, or ideally just one, consolidated opinion remaining.

6. Don't outsource the thinking. Refrain from overly relying on experts. Often there is the temptation to ask for external expert opinion (outside the team and possibly outside the company). The assumption might be that their input is reliable and relevant to the company (or team) 's specific context. Ownership must remain with the team and team leader as, even with the best intent, an outright expert cannot know all the elements of the context being considered.

7. Ensure that all individuals in the team take personal responsibility and hold themselves to account for the team's collective performance. It is not someone else's job to make the team work better, nor other people's responsibility when it comes to the results achieved and the decisions made; each team member has to ensure the team operates at the highest possible level. As Michael Jordan said, 'There is no 'I' in TEAM, but there is in WINNING.'

Pause, Reflect and Experiment: Collaborate: Alliances and Teams

(1) Do you invest in all relationships, building alliances that will endure or are you blinkered by the current hierarchy and roles?
  • How do you maintain relationships with those who are no longer within your organisation?

(2) What is the doctrine of teaming (addressing the five key questions that underpin a team's ability to perform well) for your enterprise? What are the 'rules' for coming together and performing as a team in your enterprise?

(3) Identify all the teams you are a part of (e.g., leadership teams) and those you lead or have commissioned.
  • Reflect on their current performance and how you and others may be experiencing involvement in that team.
  • What are the immediate insights into what works well and is not?

(4) Cascade is an initiative throughout the enterprise to refresh and clarify the charter for each team that is unique to each team.
  • Ensure that how each team aligns with the purposes and structures of the wider organisation is clearly understood. Who are the stakeholders, to whom is this team accountable, and where does this team get support or resources if required?

(5) Ensure that there is clarity on what type of team each team should be (i.e., how it fulfils its charter). For example, is the team to provide governance or coordination, develop ideas, and reach decisions, or is it expected to implement actions?

(6) Be precise about who is in each team and who is external but interfaces with the team.
- Are all members equally necessary and equally required to contribute to the team?
- Are all the team members held equally to account for the team's performance? Are all individuals rewarded for team performance?

(7) Do all team members of all teams in the enterprise know how they are expected to behave; has this been explicitly discussed? Do they hold each other to account (e.g., high challenge with high support, individualcommitment to this team, attention to results, reinforcing psychological safety, how decisions are made, representation from this team to the wider organisation)?
- Establish the practices and processes to track and intervene to improve team functioning during the life of the team; enhance and sustain the learning of the team and the growth of individual team members.
- Be alert to the need and opportunity to strengthen, refresh, or even rebuild the team through changes in the membership.
- Establish processes to track and reward individuals' contributions to the team's overall performance.

Chapter 7
Care: Help Others Thrive

Beyond the duty-of-care. Help others thrive.

The Well-being Imperative

Well-being is essential for performance, yet the well-being is under threat by what the World Health Organisation calls the epidemic of stress. In June 2022, *Forbes Online* led an article on well-being with the chilling headline,[53] 'Leaders are living in a well-being La-La Land'. Referencing a June 2022 report[54] by Deloitte, it went on to say, 'leaders are somewhat oblivious to not only the low levels of well-being happening with their team members but also seem to be ignoring their own personal plight.' The report by Deloitte echoes my research: executives are quitting – which is exacerbating the leadership talent crisis. Mental and emotional stress levels are too high for many. '... nearly 70% of the C-suite are seriously considering quitting for a job that better supports their well-being'.

AK: The biggest influence is personal (physical, mental, emotional, spiritual) well-being ... most things in life are based on 'what's in it for me'. If you are well – then you are a better leader. You must be centred and grounded and looking at the long term. Then you are much more able to be an effective leader. It's extremely critical [to] keep energy up [...]: physical, mental, spiritual, and financial resilience and well-being. Leaders who are resilient invest in their well-being.

MH: It's important to invest in well-being and resilience, but there's a lot of rubbish talked about it. The Michael Marmot studies* in this respect are fantastic, and the researchers who've carried it on are really impressive. What they show is that, when you work over 55 hours a week year after year, you suffer earlier cognitive decline, decline in creative and critical thinking

---

* 'The Michael Marmot studies' refers to the 'Whitehall studies'. See the article 'Health inequalities among British civil servants: the Whitehall II study.' by Prof M.G. Marmot and colleagues. It was initially published in *The Lancet* in 1991. The studies of over 10,000 staff members found significant negative health implications related to work conditions. An overriding conclusion of the report is 'Healthy behaviours should be encouraged across the whole of society; more attention should be paid to the social environments, job design, and the consequences of income inequality'.

or vocabulary loss, depression, and early onset dementia. That's medical research that everybody has turned a blind eye to. Michael Marmot did the longest-ever longitudinal study of the working conditions of Whitehall civil servants. We have built a work culture in many places where hours are considered a badge of honour, with people frequently working 80 hours. While all the medical evidence says this is really bad for you, even if you're not conscious of it, this is going to take a toll. Research shows that sleep deprivation takes an enormous toll on people's cognitive capacity. Yet we're very happy for people to fly overnight, jump into hire cars, and zoom down the motorway. However, missing a night's sleep is equivalent cognitively to being over the alcohol limit. This stuff really matters; it's not soft around the edges thinking; leaders are paid to do a physical activity, and it's done with your brain, but the way we work people mostly trashes their brains. Leaders need to think about the optimal conditions in which they can do their optimal work.

JV: Many leaders are quite fragile – as they were born into and grew their careers in more stable environments. Those of us who have been very international, particularly in developing markets, and have spent our lives in fluid, multicultural environments have an advantage. But most have not had this journey and set of experiences.

Well-being is complex, including physical, mental, financial, spiritual, and family health; it is, therefore, difficult for enterprises to support it adequately and comprehensively. Another complicating factor is that the lived reality of executives is often far from that of the employees; hence many executives are not even aware of the well-being crises their staff are struggling with – particularly financial issues. A third complicating factor is that there is much concern by human resource professionals about straying over the boundaries of personal choice. For example, providing fitness classes and supportive messages about healthy habits, healthy weight, and diet might seem positive but may negatively impact the mental well-being and the sense of inclusion of employees who are obese or otherwise unable or unwilling to participate. While companies can adopt multiple programmes, seeking to support workers with any and each of the separate areas cited above, the core approach of the enterprise should be to adopt human-centred workforce management,[55] which is the focus of Chapter 10 in my book *Management and Leadership in the 4th Industrial Revolution*. I draw the following extracts from that book.

Klaus Schwab (Executive Chairman of the World Economic Forum)[56] described the 4th Industrial Revolution as being *'more than just technology-driven change; it is an opportunity [...] to harness converging technologies to create an inclusive, human-centred future'*. It is increasingly accepted that enterprise performance depends on worker well-being – and this requires explicit investment and management.

- The World Health Organisation names an 'epidemic of stress'[57] that is spreading across populations of workers in developed countries.
- In Feb 2019, the United Nations issued a report[58] on the unsustainability of income inequality, a primary cause of the stress that erodes the mental and physical well-being of workers.

Actively Promote Well-being

As indicated above, it is increasingly understood that better well-being leads to better personal and corporate performance outcomes. As such, some enterprises appoint individuals or teams to actively promote and support aspects of well-being (particularly physical and emotional). However, such initiatives need to be curated and governed well to ensure that a well-meant initiative is not itself a cause of increased stress or anxiety for the intended beneficiaries. Many of us can probably relate to having signed up for a gym or other exercise programme only to feel intimidated when we walk in surrounded by 'buff' bodies and confronted by the intensity of the trainer urging us to do 'just ten more!'

BJ: Firms have been weighing on physical health – but now they are getting involved in mental health issues. Positive [aspects include] mindfulness, meditation, [and the] ability to grow – firms are also leaning into the negative [aspects]: anxiety, stress, depression, etc. This leads to lots of 'danger areas' – especially across genders, e.g., one CEO said to an executive, 'You need to lose significant weight and take care of yourself.' The CEO is right – but is it legal? Is it pressure?

CE: [The] ability to lead through turbulent times [involves] sustainability of leadership and organisation through crises.

PC: Mid-career breaks are very important – as we live and work longer. We need to find better ways of balancing our lives. We can't work ceaselessly. A mid-life MOT is also very good. We must expect people/help people to take real breaks – go and learn something new or go and meditate – don't just sit on a beach – do something meaningful – sail around the world, etc. Don't make it too formulaic – not just at a set time of life. Creating a glide/slope into retirement is more important than the 'cliff'.

In 2015, the United Nations (UN) adopted the 17 goals for sustainable development, with the aspiration that they are all achieved by 2030. Goal 3 is to ensure healthy lives and promote well-being for all at all ages. However, according to research[59] 9by Josh Bersin, in April 2021, there were over 55,000 vacancies in the US alone for 'well-being' managers.

Enable Others to Thrive

The ability to attract, develop and retain talent[60] is a differentiator of corporate performance. This factor is forecast to become increasingly important as the rate of job dislocation and the need for upskilling and reskilling at pace continue to accelerate. Employees and contract workers have increasing agency when their skills are in demand, while they also recognise that, to remain relevant, they must engage in constant upskilling. As such, enabling others to thrive (well-being) and to develop skills can help enterprises to win the 'war for talent'.

BJ: Team members must believe that they are in the best place for them to develop and thrive. They have to feel that you are operating in their best interests. [Then] they feel they are going to get a lot out of it.

IS: If you can't develop them, then you can't lead.

TM: I want to help the people around me be the best they can be.

SGJ: The leader is responsible for positively impacting each person for the future – beyond when we are together! Maybe 20 years later – they will realise the positivity of the experience with me. It's all about people.

JV: Increasingly, leading is teaching others – not just mentoring – it needs to be more structured now. You must have 'skin in the game' of their development and success.

In the book *Drive: The Surprising Truth About What Motivates Us*,[61] Daniel Pink outlines his findings on helping others to thrive. He describes a mix of Autonomy, Mastery and Purpose.

- **Autonomy:** Giving sufficient autonomy to the people you manage boosts their creativity. In addition, they will seek more responsibility, allowing you to delegate more tasks to them. By offering your employees greater choices, you will give them the freedom they need to be motivated and encouraged to propose new projects to you.

- **Mastery:** Help others master what they are doing and perform feedback cycles in which you highlight what they have done well and what remains to be done to reach the next level. Offer the necessary training. An employee who has mastered his environment and work will tend to propose additional things that will benefit the company.

- **Purpose:** You must be able to bring out the purpose of what you are trying to accomplish on a daily basis for your employees. They must know and be inspired by the purpose of what they do daily. Their efforts need to make sense.

To these three principles, I would add two more.

1. When motivating others, it is helpful to understand how they think so that you can approach them most effectively. Seek to understand their personality type, e.g., through one or other of the neuroscience frameworks such as David Rock's SCARF[62] model or the Myers-Briggs[63] personality type indicator. Some personality types require greater clarity on the expectations and specific goals, while others are comfortable with only knowing how their efforts align with the wider purpose of the organisation.

2. Reinforcement through praise, reward and recognition is extremely important for maintaining motivation and energy. It could be as simple as commenting 'well done' but that still provides significant emotional income to the recipient. Sir Alex Ferguson noted:[64] 'For a player – for any human being – there is nothing better than hearing "Well done." Those are the two best words ever invented. You don't need to use superlatives.'

Create a Culture of Care and Support

'Culture is the glue that binds an organisation together. It has a very significant impact on the firm's effectiveness, ethics, and governance. How could a board not have a view on the fitness-for-purpose of the firm's culture?'[65]

Sir Adrian Montague, former Chairman of Aviva plc.

Organisation culture defines how we do things and why they are done that way. There is a common identity and understanding of how to interact regarding behavioural norms and mindsets. A productive culture enables individuals to collaborate effectively with one another, increasing employee retention and engagement—an unproductive culture results in mistrust, low engagement and difficulties in collaboration and cooperation. A very poor culture can lead to breakdowns in ethics, which creates legal jeopardy and reputational risk.

IS: You can be as analytical about the culture as you can be about the balance sheet – e.g., the way people engage with problems and with each other, taking risks, exposing themselves and their vulnerabilities. There needs to be a learning culture – not a blame and fear culture.

PC: Examples exist where there is a culture about sharp elbows. I think this is not the best way to get the best out of people: lots of politics, churn and burn-out. It creates unpredictability about how things work – which will come around and bite you. If people don't trust each other, there may be an inner circle that holds power and keeps great, new talent on the outside, unable to do their job. Sadly, however, there are lots of examples where this gets rewarded.

PC2: Understanding culture and behaviour is super important now. When the culture is right, we collaborate well, and people want to work for us.

NH: The culture we needed to be about was ownership and taking action – rather than waiting to be told what to do. Covid helped the culture shift – people had to stand up and be counted – and change habits.

Although living the culture is the responsibility of every member of the enterprise, the roles played by the board of directors, top team and supervisors are particularly important. The top team and supervisors are the role models whose behaviour is observed and mirrored throughout the organisation. The standards that they hold themselves to or 'let slip' are the norms that others adopt. The board is critical, as the culture defines the enterprise's performance conditions. Governance of the culture is essential to reduce performance, legal and reputational risks.

People Management: Put the Human Back in Human Resource Management

Talent is a critical, scarce resource that requires careful management using head and heart. Human Centered Workforce Management is increasingly recognised as a priority, and Chief People Officers often included in the most senior leadership team. Human Centered Workforce Management (HCWM) is the adoption of practices that cherish and nurture people, fulfilling the spirit, not only the legal obligations, of the duty of care.

MH: Take yourself lightly but take leadership seriously. First and foremost, you are responsible to those around you who are choosing to work with you, giving hours, days, or years of their lives to help you achieve the goals and vision you have set out. Do everything that you can to repay their faith and trust in you. Build them up, increase their skills and confidence and help them achieve their goals, to look after their health and care for their family members.

CU: There's a distinct difference between a people director who sits on the board and is respected as an equal member – and those organisations that have HR as a must-have rather than a 'want-to-have'. The traditionalists focus on compliance to minimise legal risk; they want to maximise the power of the employer, make employees interchangeable and ensure staff costs are as low as possible. The modern people director sees people as THE core asset of the enterprise, endlessly reconfigurable and highly productive so long as you keep developing future-relevant skills, enable each person to flourish and fluidly deploy the best talent to the most important initiatives.

1. **Job Churn**. A key aspect of HCWM is supporting workers through the turbulence of the churn that is occurring in the labour market. As previously mentioned, it is expected that there will a 23% churn in the labour market[66] and that 44% of workers' skills will be disrupted in the five years to 2028. In this context, many individuals will be anxious about their jobs and the future relevance of their skill sets. People managers must help their staff navigate this turmoil, enabling everyone who wants, to reskill at the pace they want, to proactively support staff whose jobs are changing and to help others transition to new roles if theirs are being displaced.

ML: What is very repeatable can be easily done by AI – whereas EQ and creativity are domains of humans – and therefore, leaders will increasingly need to be experts with humans – and know how to lead people who are strong in technology spaces.

KC: The population is bifurcating – many will not be able to keep up. So, we are moving faster towards [a situation where] winners-take-all. You will either have the skills or not. I fear an increasing split between those with the skills to generate wealth and those who increasingly get left out.

2. **Flexible Working Arrangements.** In many countries, worker expectations and statutory conditions are extending the working life. In part, this is due to extending life expectancy, and partly, it is due to the failure of pension systems. Four-generation workforces are increasingly common. In this context, individuals transition through many life stages during their careers, with each life stage placing different constraints and obligations on their time and energies. A worker may be juggling care for young children or care for ailing elderly parents with their work commitments. They may be suffering from health issues or managing a second job to generate sufficient income. A recent CIPD report[67] notes, 'Flexible working isn't equally important for everyone. At any time, evidence suggests most employees are prepared to go along with existing norms for how work is organised – or, generally, improvements to this aspect of their working lives are not a high priority. But for some employees, at various points in their working lives, flexible working is of much greater importance and value; it can perhaps be essential to them participating in paid employment at all.'

SW: People struggling to achieve a living wage experience high anxiety and stress; this may be amplified by income insecurity through the low contract hours and flexible working arrangements our company is implementing, so should we pay everyone more? Employees also seek supplementary income by taking on additional jobs with flexible working arrangements; should we provide as much certainty as possible on the hours we require to help them plan their other jobs around ours?

3. **Boundary Management.** Each person has their preferred way of perceiving the interplay of their personal and work domains. At one extreme are individuals ('segmenters') who prefer to maintain a separation between work and family domains. At the other extreme are individuals ('integrators') who prefer to

integrate the two domains. This difference in outlook determines a large part of how an individual experiences the benefits and negatives of increased boundary blurring. For individuals preferring a high degree of separation, increased work-related activities in their personal time contribute to anxiety and stress, as do interruptions to their working time caused by personal life or family members. Whereas integrators, who prefer to overlap personal and worktime, feel anxiety and stress when they are forced to be in one or another mode (for instance, wondering, 'Have my children reached home OK?' while they are at work, or 'Did we get confirmation on the contract in Tokyo?' while at dinner in New York).

4. **I-Deals and Job Crafting:** Increasingly, managers are required to have the skills, awareness, and authority to establish individual arrangements with staff members, i.e., not constrained by standardised job description 'boxes', compensation formulae and working arrangement policies. I-deals (idiosyncratic work arrangements) and job-crafting[68] are 'voluntary, personalised agreements of a non-standard nature negotiated between individual employees and their employers regarding terms that benefit each party'[69].Job crafting tends to develop organically, driven by the employee adapting the way they do their work or extending beyond the formal boundaries of their role. The employer then accommodates but does not formalise the arrangement. Idiosyncratic* arrangements (I-Deals[70]) tend to be formalised arrangements which have been negotiated. There are four principal types of I-deals:

   • **Task:** Arrangements that aim to contribute to how employees carry out tasks, for example, allowing the use of special (or personal) equipment.

   • **Career:** Any deals that aim to develop one's career and lead to advancements, for example, a dispensation to join a specialist task force.

   • **Flexibility:** Individual arrangements that relate to flexibilities in terms of time and location of work.

   • **Financial:** Arrangements relating to salary negotiations, promotions, perks, and other monetary terms.

BJ: The big trend that's happening now is that knowledge workers have power (Drucker also said this). The pandemic has accelerated this. These workers

---

* Idiosyncratic deals, or i-deals, are the individualised working arrangements negotiated by employees with the organisations for which they work. Such deals represent an emerging area of study into the effects they have on both parties, as well as co-workers and the wider working world

require flexible working conditions, including location; if you don't offer it, then they will easily work for someone else who will. This is not only an issue for a large company, say, in Seattle, when their talent wants to move to New York, but is also an issue for a 'family owned' company in, say, Nebraska, when their talent can now be poached by the global company in Seattle, which no longer requires the staff to relocate from Nebraska and will pay them Seattle rates.

So, as a leader, I need to be very altruistic. I want a strong team, but they have lots of power. I need to treat everyone as an individual (as they each want different things) – but with a fair process, and they can be anywhere in the world. This is a critical skill for leaders to manage.

In my era, you would go to work and then fit in the social and personal stuff around that, but now folks figure out their weekly social schedule – and then they wrap the work around those obligations! It's a complete flip. The framing is completely different. You cannot have a set of job description boxes and traditional HR approaches to accommodate this workforce; you have to have idiosyncratic deals. Leaders have more stress now – as only they can figure out the individual deals – HR cannot.

SG: What the pandemic did was to make every business realise how much they were reliant on the individuals inside the organisation for their survival; it wasn't the tech, it wasn't the brilliant product … they had to respond to unpredictable circumstances with all their ingenuity and creativity and collaboration inside the company. […] it's ever more apparent that your ability to create the conditions in which individuals can flourish inside and outside your organisation is going to be the main factor; [it will define] whether you're going actually to survive or not. So, mediocrity and not paying attention to that stuff is just instant death or a lot quicker than it used to be.

The Leader's Role in Implementing HCWM

Remove doubt. Clarify the support available. Make it clear by establishing the infrastructure (physical, policies and systems) to promote well-being and overtly establish and promote a supportive culture within the firm. It may include family caregiver days, flexible days off, well-being services/facilities provided in-house or nearby, or external speakers and classes. Establish and clearly communicate policies and expectations on flexible and mobile working, activities that promote well-being, and the ability to manage the work/family-life boundary.

Allow choice and flexibility. Make it clear that each individual can make their own choices about how they fit within the boundaries of the initiatives, events or activities established by the employer. For example, if an individual has booked into a wellness class during the traditional working day or at lunchtime and is then asked to respond to a request from their manager, is it acceptable to delay responding until after the class?

Enrol supervisors. By itself, adopting a set of guidelines does little to change ingrained behaviours and practices. Even if adopted as an explicit policy, it is still essential to shape the firm's culture through nurturing appropriate behaviours, particularly the role modelling demonstrated by team leaders and supervisors. Training and monitoring the behaviour of such leaders, particularly regarding their support for managing the work/family-life boundary, positively impact employee engagement and productivity and has been proven to significantly benefit employee health, job satisfaction, and turnover intentions.[71]

BJ: As leaders, we need to role-model investment in the well-being of others and ourselves. But this leads to many 'danger areas' – especially across genders. Perhaps someone has just lost a spouse or had a baby with a severe illness; do you give them extra time off as they struggle to deal with it? Is this policy just because they asked for it or because they seemed to be struggling? Do you not give the time off to someone who seems to be functioning well despite their loss or similar situation? What about if the one struggling is female and the one seemingly functioning well is male? Are you gender-biased in your treatment? Leaders have more stress now – as only they can figure out the individual deals – HR cannot.

Role model. The leader's own behaviour is a powerful role model that must be within the established guidelines and demonstrate exercising personal choice. Leaders also must promote well-being, role-modelling in their behaviours to boost and protect their well-being, and proactively support others. Arianna Huffington, the founder of Thrive Global, underscores the importance of role-modelling:[72] 'We believe that when leaders take care of themselves, they are much more able to take care of their employees to be empathetic, creative, and inspiring. But when they're depleted, running on empty and burnt out, it's much harder to lead from what is best in them.'

Every leader should reflect on their own and the executive team's people management skills. Gather feedback from staff members across the enterprise and during exit discussions with leavers. Also, reflect on whether key staff members have followed you between teams, companies, or countries as your career has evolved.

RC: Remember the people, not the HR policy – the people.

CM: Good leaders need to be great at coaching, empowering, getting teams to excel and be motivated … and less reliant on traditional HR tools – not top-down ones, not just standard rewards/metrics, etc.

LB: People are, and will always be, at heart, individuals with different characteristics and personalities.

Competitive advantage or disadvantage results from the ability of the enterprise to attract, deploy, develop, and retain key talent with future-relevant skills. Many of the mindsets and approaches described in this book contribute to overall HCWM – for example, connecting with and motivating others (including those not like 'me'), helping others to thrive, and allowing flexibility within guidelines.

Beyond the Duty of Care

Some of the panellists who are overtly conscious of the obligation to care for their followers, even speak of a sense of love and compassion that far surpasses a contractual relationship or the legal duty-of-care.

PC: Genuinely know and care about those you are trying to lead – people no longer have patience with remote leaders (if they ever did). If you don't care about them and are not interested in their success, why will they be loyal, committed, or interested in you and what you are trying to achieve? Eat last within sight of the men – make sure they know you care.

SB: Respect them as individuals who have a life outside of work. More and more, we have to understand, empathise and lean in when our team members are having challenges. Lean in and support them – or even get them professional help when/if required. There is a blurring of the boundary between professional and private life. This was necessary during the pandemic – which normalised authenticity. But this continues now. The boundaries are blurred. Truly [provide] authentic, good leadership – genuinely caring for each team member.

JV: Caring – people need to know that you care about them – that you are genuinely interested in them – that you are thoughtful about the business and how folks who come along will benefit from that journey with you. Why should they be spending time with you on this journey? For example, I flew to a team member's funeral in mid-trip – it was the right thing to do, and I cared about him. Being there meant something, not talking about it – not sending a 'care package' but going and being there in person.

MH: Take leadership (leading others) really seriously; take yourself less seriously. Leading others is a great responsibility. For yourself, have fun, and learn. Build the foundation based on nurturing and building others.

RP: The traditional notion of a managerial 'duty of care' has expanded significantly in its remit, definition and employee expectation.

AJ: Help people be better people, lifting each other up, helping them understand their lives and the choices they make and can make. People should know what we stand for, and there should be no doubt about that, either for them or for us as leaders, ourselves.

Although only a handful of the leaders I have worked with use the label 'servant leadership' (which I introduced in Chapter 4 as a form of values-based leadership), a sizable proportion of the panellists describe the attitude and actions of caring for others that reflect the concept. To recap: a servant leader[73] focuses primarily on the growth and well-being of people and the communities to which they belong. While traditional leadership generally involves the accumulation and exercise of power by one person at the 'top of the pyramid', servant leadership shares power, puts the needs of others first and helps people develop and perform as highly as possible.'[74]

Resurgence of Employee Ownership

For the past 40 years, we have witnessed the increase in the wealth gap between workers and owners, in significant part driven by the policies of employers to manage labour costs and benefits. Now there is a rebalancing of the relationship between employee and employer as talent (with 4th Industrial Revolution-relevant skills) is in short supply, chooses where to work and is prepared to switch employers. Talent seeks ways to cross the wealth gap and to connect with roles and entities with greater purpose. Increasingly such talent is also seeking a share of ownership, expecting to be included in leadership discussions and to benefit from future liquidity events and the venture's success.

KH: Employees understand profit and want to have a fair share ... there will be much more inclusive ways that profits and value creation (e.g., through shares) are shared with employees – or more individuals will work for themselves, choosing contracts and companies that give them the income they need.

AI: We will need to work on ensuring that your team is more invested in the success and mission of the organisation: e.g., being given equity (perhaps like John Lewis Partnership or Richer Sounds). We will need to grant people a bigger stake in the organisation. Talent is so important – if that is the case, then surely the team needs to be more invested in the organisation, benefiting from the success they generate. Senior leadership should not be the sole beneficiary of firm performance. It will be a product of the tighter talent market. The employee ownership principle will become more important – people having a genuine emotional and financial stake in the business's success – a new psychological pact between the business and the team members (not employees). We will also see the abolition of gender and ethnicity pay gaps – talent is talent.

Pause, Reflect and Experiment: Care: Help Others Thrive

(1) Do you prioritise your well-being? Are you living as a role model for others? (Health, family, emotion, spiritual). What are you doing for your well-being? If it's not important for you, it is unlikely that you will make it a priority for those around you.
   • What are your enterprise's well-being initiatives, support, communications, and other signalling?

(2) Are you actively seeking to enable all individuals to be the best version of themselves so that they can be well and make their best contributions?
   • What is the evidence of your actions that positively support individuals?

(3) Build into each day the discipline to support others AND your well-being.
- Role model: Be conscious of how you influence the team (enterprise) culture through your behaviour and words.
- Identify ways to support and encourage staff enterprise-wide to emulate positive culture-building behaviours.

(4) Build community: Enhance the sense of community and belonging between all team/staff members.
- Focus on the purpose, values and superordinate goals that bring people together.
- Celebrate successes and life events with one another and support each other in setbacks.

(5) Support job crafting and I-deals: When appropriate for an individual, explore ways to flex the job scope or the requirements for how the job is executed to enhance their ability and motivation to exceed expectations for their role (I-deals and job crafting).
- How can you bring individual job customisation to the organisation without creating undue complexity and ensuring transparency and fairness?
- Celebrate and highlight successful examples.

(6) Encourage, enable, and recognise upskilling and reskilling achievements of all employees throughout the enterprise.
- Support self-directed learning.
- Encourage learning in the flow of work, i.e., on-demand, not just scheduled cohorts in recognised programmes.
- Recognise and reward development accomplishments (e.g., through inclusion in priority projects and career acceleration opportunities)

PART FOUR
Adapt

Increase the Dynamic Capacity of the enterprise and the mobility of resources. 'Adaptable' emphasises the capacity to adjust and change as needed, even if the adjustments are substantial, while 'agile' places more emphasis on speed, flexibility, and the ability to navigate change through iterative processes.

Flex: Dynamic Capacity

Sustainable advantage is the ability to repeatedly move between transient positions of advantage.

Today's leaders must increase the capacity to adapt, to flex, the enterprise. Much like a professional tennis player performing at the top of their game, agility is not a substitute for having a strategy; instead, adaptability is the capability that enables an intended strategy to be implemented whilst also responding to the evolving situation. The more unpredictable the competitor and changes in the weather conditions, the more the player must adapt to win. The capability of an enterprise to adapt as the context and competitors evolve is known as the Dynamic Capacity. The stock prices of publicly traded companies with a higher-than-average dynamic capacity outperform the stocks of their industry-sector peers by over 30% (over five years).[75] Whereas the stock prices of those companies with below-average dynamic capacity underperform their sector peers by approx. 15%. The ability to adapt, to flex the enterprise, is more important the faster changing, less predictable the context and competitors.

PC: The world that was – in which we were successful – is no longer here. Leaders cannot become more risk-averse. All decisions have risks; moving too slowly and cautiously is perhaps a greater risk. We must embrace and understand that risk is required, being adaptive, Agile, responsive, and resilient.

MH: We've always taught management as a sort of three-legged stool, which is forecast, plan, execute, but we're now living in an environment where forecasts have little validity. It is a very different terrain from the one we're used to, and it's completely at odds with the one that we might have studied. Traditionally, since the industrial revolution, our guiding principle has been efficiency, but now it is quite dangerous. As you can't really see where you're going, then when you're very efficient, and some surprise jumps out at you, you have no margin with which to change. You can't pursue only just in time; it's too vulnerable to surprises. Going back is not an option, as what you thought was 'normal' is now history. You need a mindset and very different organising principles and people around you. You need to be highly imaginative, which the traditional model of leaders isn't. You have to prepare multiple options, and really quickly, you have to understand in a different way who you need help from so you make the right decisions, and your decision-making process makes them look and feel legitimate.

RB: You are now unlikely to have a period of 4–5 years without instability – this is quite different to the context of leaders previously.

AB: Ultimately, the success of a leader is their ability to keep the business proposition relevant while maximising the value for all stakeholders. For this, constant innovation and responsible leadership are the secret sauce of success.

RP: New thinking and ways of working are required, which can be an existential challenge for traditional corporates or large family-owned businesses. Many businesses are still operating in a very analogue world, delivering real-life goods and services where excess speed of change can undermine customer, consumer, and employee confidence. Being too slow to adapt makes them look old-fashioned, unappealing, and irrelevant. Even acknowledging this paradox can sometimes be challenging in a corporate environment. Leaders need to make practical and emotional space to hear 'inconvenient truths' and recognise the Cassandras in their teams, value them for their challenge, and tolerate them for their perceived disruption. Adapt to survive, be agile to thrive.

NH: Flow – create the sense of flow; how do we drive agility in the organisation? Companies that win are those that move fastest. Efficiency is a foundational requirement; it is not a differentiator any longer.

The capacity to act dynamically is determined by the 'multiplication' of the strength of three sets of capabilities.[76]

(1) The capability to 'Sense and Make Sense' of the unfolding situation. To see and understand what is happening and how the elements we observe will likely come together.
  • What is the 'play' that is about to unfold?

(2) The capability to 'Seize and Replicate', to identify and decide what to do and implement rapidly across the enterprise.
  • How are we responding to the 'play' as it unfolds?

(3) The capability to 'Reconfigure' the activities and 'Reposition' the business models and offerings of the enterprise.
  • How do we position ourselves to execute better now and as the match continues?

Creating and using Dynamic Capacity requires leadership, establishing an enterprise-wide view, driving the creation and strengthening of the mechanisms that enable each of the three sets of capabilities and then being able to draw all three together to enable planning, decision making and pushing through implementation. The benefits are clear, but to wield Dynamic Capacity the leader requires high credibility, as they must flex the enterprise despite the inherent bias of all organisations to refine the 'as is'.

Pause, Reflect and Experiment: Flex: Dynamic Capacity

(1) What is the level of dynamic capacity in your enterprise? Take the online assessment and compare and discuss the results with colleagues.
   • Note: A free online assessment questionnaire, which provides an immediate e-mail report comparing your responses to the population of companies surveyed, can be found at http://www.corporaterebirth.com/.

(2) Is the current level of dynamic capacity sufficient (and providing an advantage over your competitors) for the rate of change and flux in your marketspaces today and into the future?

(3) Discuss the need to be adaptive, flexing as the future unfolds – being adaptive in a timely manner is good leadership; demonstrate the need to revisit forecasts and plans and undertake such reviews with structure and balanced argument.

(4) Identify priorities and the specific actions that you can implement to strengthen the dynamic capabilities:
   • Capabilities to Sense and Make Sense.
   • Capabilities to Seize and Replicate.
   • Capabilities to Reconfigure and Reposition.

(5) Determine specific actions to improve the integration across the three sets of dynamic capabilities.
   • Does the leadership team act in ways that reinforce rigidity (e.g., department and business unit budgets, resources, and deviation from plan) or ways that leverage and improve dynamic capacity (i.e., increasing the strategic and operational adaptability of the enterprise), increasing performance of the whole enterprise?

Chapter 8
Build Capabilities to Sense and Make Sense

Knowing what's next is more valuable than what's now.

The skills of sensing (what's unfolding) and making sense (seeing how the factors will combine to create specific threats and opportunities) are essential for an enterprise to thrive in today's turbulent context.

Leaders need to gather insights, and snippets of data, broadly. There is no competitive advantage achieved from waiting on an industry report to be published, especially in a fast-evolving sector. Instead, gather 'idea fragments' from people across the organisation and externally whilst also monitoring news and information 'feeds'. An 'idea fragment' is a snippet of news, an observation, a partially formed thought or a piece of data. Idea fragments have no value by themselves. When combined with others (connecting the dots) a picture of what is happening or what you might do is revealed that could be of great value. Steve Jobs is quoted as saying, 'more dots, better dots', i.e., collect more and more relevant idea fragments, and then your interrogation of them will reveal more.

- Involve your whole team (or workforce); imbue them with a common purpose.
- Strive to counteract cognitive biases such as recency, location, cognitive or selection biases.
- Regularly interrogate the growing database of idea fragments.

MH: We're seeing the rise of open strategy because there's an understanding that there's more knowledge at the edge of the companies than the centre. [When you are] involving them more directly, they know what's going on much more than you do in the centre. How do you know which of those people to convene around which questions? You can't convene everybody on everything all the time! How do you understand the population watching you make these decisions and ensure that they understand them and trust the process by which they've been made?

HM: The only way you can sense what's going on out there is if the population within your company looks like the population beyond your company. That's now a business risk if everyone is similar inside the company because they're not in touch with what society looks like. That may make them happier and make it a lot easier to do business because people, broadly speaking, think the same way, but it means that the chances of being blindsided are increased.

RP: Fight to get external input, inspiration and ideas. Develop the habit of attending external events virtually or in person and collecting examples of great service. What made it great? Think beyond that final-stage interaction you had and try and imagine backwards into their organisation and all the steps it took to get that final delivery right. What can you learn and challenge your organisation on? How will you go about challenging the status quo effectively?

AI: Be really aware of what your competition is doing – while knowing that the most dangerous competition is the competition you don't know – the ntrepreneurs and innovators that you don't yet recognise. I need to be paranoid; this mindset must drive the innovation flywheel.

JA: The need to be agile along many more dimensions than previously required. In this hyper-connected era, where five–ten-year strategic planning may be obsolete due to rapidly changing technological, societal and economic shifts and your workforce/content experts are likely to be decentralised, global agility becomes a critically differentiating factor for today's leaders. I experienced this when I relocated to Asia to run the [...]. My ability to be agile [comes] from the perspective of dealing in a region with wide cultural differences that translate into how work is done and geographical challenges that require differing go-to-market strategies based on environmental, infrastructure and social differences; all of these [were] underpinned by the human element of motivating a diverse workforce subject to the socio-economic and general issues seen in each country (now spread across the most populous region on the planet!). It tested my [ability to Sense and Make Sense] to the maximum. It took me years to say that I developed the muscles needed to become effective enough at meeting this challenge.

Proactively ask colleagues and others you meet to expand on their observations and to share their thinking with you. You don't have to agree that they are right, but you do want to benefit from understanding what they are seeing and how they are thinking. Push them to say more: ' *... and what have you seen, why did that get your attention, what do you think that could mean for us?*'

SG: The ability to listen to people who are impacted by business decisions is really critical. Of course, the employees, but also the customers and communities in which we're operating, suppliers and investors, and literally everybody that the business touches. If you're listening to other people, you're much more humble and will learn faster.

TC: You need to have the skill to ask questions in 360-degree arcs; for example, asking how prepared we are for the forthcoming challenges of technological advances. [You also need to be] asking the right probing questions of 'Are we ready?' and ''How can we embrace this?'

CE: Listening skills – and having the opportunities to listen – create these opportunities and develop the skills.

ML: Listening more [with] not so much broadcasting. Take time to understand other people and why they think what they think. People are more active and expect to be participating in the debate. It is impossible now to tell people what to do – individuals make their own choices and are unwilling to accept what they are told.

Adopt an approach of rapid experimentation, perform 'tests' to probe and learn about the market, customer behaviour, competitor actions, technology, etc. The approach seeks to cause a reaction to the test' initiative so that you can accelerate your learning. It can be aided by adopting the mindset of ready-fire-aim (rather than ready-aim-fire) to increase the speed and breadth of experimentation – the 'aim' (understanding how to craft a potential solution) only occurs when we have built the understanding of the market, competitors, technology etc. Conduct multiple test-to-learn experiments in parallel, intending to learn and adjust from each. Then you can combine insights together into a potential new offering that becomes the subject of a pilot test.

AI: Move really fast on innovation cycles (maybe design thinking or lean start-up). Test new ideas, move quickly, learn and retest.

JH: Encourage risk-taking and accept mistakes to learn faster.

Heighten Situational Awareness

Situational awareness is mainly associated with security and sporting contexts, where it has long been expected that changes could happen quickly and from unexpected, as well as expected, players and adversaries. However, with heightened uncertainty and increased instability and rate of change, situational awareness is increasingly garnering attention in the business context. Situational awareness involves monitoring a broad array of actors and circumstances to seek to understand what is unfolding before it has happened and to respond to opportunities or threats pre-emptively, or at least in a timely manner so that your objectives are furthered.

IS: Leaders must have high situational awareness – [of] all the complex forces around them. [You] must be alert to all these forces impinging on you. [You] must have a broader view of what is happening.

CU: Situational awareness is the first thing that allows people to stay ahead of the curve; spend enough time keeping your head up. Situational awareness has relevance in self-leadership, but it is at the organisational level that it makes a huge difference to performance. Situational awareness is the lens through which to make good quality decisions. All other characteristics mean nothing if someone doesn't have situational awareness. They need to be good at looking up and looking ahead when others look down and at the problems.

   Situational awareness is the first thing that allows people to stay ahead of the curve, spending enough time keeping their heads up.

BS: Be careful of following the 3–5-year plan with blinkers on – rather, have the plan and then listen to customers and staff. Constantly seek to improve.

RP: Leaders have to have their foot permanently switching between the brake and accelerator like a go-kart driver, constantly making minor adjustments with the steering wheel while accelerating forward, glancing only occasionally backwards to see where the next competitor is coming from.

Discern Signal from Noise

'Signal' is important; it carries a message about the unfolding situation that the leader should notice and respond to. However, there are so many messages, data sources, conflicting actions, and opinions that it is impossible to stay abreast of them all and give sufficient attention to them to determine their veracity and importance; there's too much 'noise'. It is estimated that the data generation and collection rate doubles every 18–24 months. That's a lot of data, too much. MIT estimates that companies analyse less than 0.5% of available data; it's easier to collect and store data than it is to interrogate it and produce insights for action. We are 'data rich and insight poor'. There isn't the time or capacity to constantly interrogate all data hoping that new insights and ideas will emerge. As managers, we need to filter out the noise and tune in to the signals that matter. First deciding what questions, we are looking to answer and then collecting and monitoring the data we think is most relevant. However, by so doing, we create confirmation biases and reduce the opportunity to see the unexpected. The leader must stand apart from such processes, instead noticing and probing anomalies and asking creative questions of the data.

CS: Given the increasing rate of change and the significant amount of information being generated in the digital space, another important attribute is being able to discern information from noise.

HW: You must be able to see what is going on – to have the helicopter quality.

DL: Discernment is key in this period. Like in Daoism, [there is] no black and white. Empower your followers to believe that what you are doing and deciding is right – they may have different opinions, but if they believe you are taking decisions with discernment of the situation, they will follow. Just look at Tesla, which almost failed – but is now highly in demand. You must have faith in your mission and have 'no guilt' that you have always made decisions in pursuit of that mission. You may have to sacrifice the company's [shorter-term] profits in pursuit of the mission.

IS: Have a great strategy – clear strategic thinking, short-term initiatives linked to the strategy. It's much more than the vision and the mission. Bring it down to what to do tomorrow – with objectives and metrics. I've developed a 'critical five' things that we focus on – which have many sub-initiatives below them – but these five priorities have been effective for energising, communicating and holding each person to account.

Improve Judgement

Judgement takes over when certainty gives up. Leaders must make judgement calls. If there were a certainty, it would be the duty of a manager, an executive tasked with analysis and drawing out conclusions. Judgement exists because not all the facts are known or can be known. The future interactions and interdependencies in the complex system surrounding your business and market space cannot be modelled or known. Leaders must be comfortable making judgement-based decisions.

DL: You must have judgement. There are always different potential solutions, different people you can work with, different ways of governing and managing the relationship, and different timings for action; they may all have equal merit. To move forward, you need to have judgement.

PM Judgement can be developed through experiential training; this is the only way to develop it. Some foundations may come from books and case studies, but the best ones come from being in the situation – intuitive judgement. The breadth of experience is, therefore, critical. We must accelerate giving people experience, e.g., shortening their spell in a single post – giving faster, shorter assignments – with a greater variety of contexts, not only roles. How can we compress the training time without diluting the experience? The number one requirement for leadership success now is to be comfortable with ambiguity. The ability to take timely decisions, without all the information, without certainty – requires comfort and capability of judgement.

Judgement can be developed, but it takes hard work and effort, and first, we need to understand how judgement works and why it is so often flawed. In his excellent book *Thinking Fast and Slow*[77] the Nobel Prize winner, Daniel Kahneman, explains how judgement happens and why we are so beset with unconscious biases and heuristics: shortcuts in our thinking that, unfortunately, can often lead us astray.

Kahneman describes two competing systems within our minds which enable us to make decisions.

- **System 1** is fast-thinking, automatic, instinctive, and emotionally driven by intuition and impulses. It relies on mental shortcuts that generate intuitive answers to problems as they arise. System 1 operates quickly with no sense of voluntary control.

- **System 2** is slow-thinking; it is logical and deliberate and tends to be more rational and analytical. System 2 deals with effortful mental activity of any kind.

We avoid cognitive overload by breaking up current tasks into small steps to be committed to long-term memory; we are naturally drawn to solutions that use as little mental effort as possible. A hard task completed once using System 2 thinking is codified as heuristics for future use by System 1. Still, System 1 is insensitive to the quality and the quantity of the information on which the heuristic is used in the future, which can lead to flawed judgement and risk-taking. Often System 1 takes in information and reaches correct conclusions nearly effortlessly using intuition and rules of thumb, for example when we are still able to make out the meaning of a piece of dialogue even though the signal is intermittent or corrupted – our System 1 helps us 'fill in the blanks', but we might, later on, discover that we have made some gross errors by assuming we did hear correctly. System 2 thinking can help us spot when our intuition is wrong or our emotions have clouded our judgement and correct poor snap judgements. Still, trying to engage System 2 in every situation and aspect of our life is exhausting and time-consuming. Kahneman says that the way to block errors that arise from System 1 is to recognise the signs that you are in a 'cognitive minefield' – i.e., to be familiar with types of situations and choices where the heuristics and biases will likely trip us up. Forewarned is forearmed.

Understanding how we make judgements and being on alert for situations where we could easily make a wrong call due to the inappropriate application of a heuristic so that we can think more methodically is a key foundation for better decision-making. In addition, we can adopt a few helpful practices. Leaders often face dilemmas without clarity; they must decide based on their values and purpose, which requires having these firmly established as described in Part 2.

Pause, Reflect and Experiment: Build Capabilities to Sense and Make Sense

(1) How good are you today, as an individual and as the leadership team, in seeing the situation as it is and as it is unfolding?
   - Do you receive multiple flows of insight and opinion? Deliberately challenge incumbent's blinkers and group-think blind spots. Involve others in wading through the data, distilling meaning and generating insights and implications.

(2) Which of the three fallacies of planning[78] might you be susceptible to?
   - The fallacy of prediction (i.e., you believe that a forecast is accurate and should be adhered to, even when shown not to be).
   - The fallacy of process (i.e., you hold each other to the numbers in the plan, despite encountering unknown opportunities and challenges).
   - The fallacy of detachment (i.e., as the future is unknown and forecasts are always inaccurate, why to bother to assert any view, instead be as responsive and agile as possible).

(3) Heighten situational awareness.
- Look more broadly at what is happening in the market space and beyond. Give yourself space and time to pause, reflect, make sense, and find the signal.
- Monitor data for signals, and turn down the noise.
- Investigate anomalies to increase understanding and awareness.

(4) Improve judgement. Practice using techniques that slow down your thinking and help you make deliberate decisions.
- Create emotional distance between yourself and the situation- you are more likely to spot and challenge biases or a dangerous moment to apply a heuristic. One approach is to 'pause', think briefly about the broader context and then re-examine the information and options. Question to what extent the information is reliable and representative and whether there are other options. If you cannot create emotional distance for yourself, ask someone else, a trusted but dispassionate confidante, to give you some reflections or observations.
- Establish processes and techniques that always challenge the emergent proposal or interpretation of the situation, such that there is no stigma attached to the person or the act of dissent and challenge. For example, for every proposition, there must be a counter-proposition that, if true, nullifies the original proposal. So, a proposal can only go through if someone else has argued thoughtfully against it. Ensure that there is cognitive diversity in the team that discusses the issue.
- Seek to identify the personal interests that might be positively or negatively impacted by the people discussing or making the proposal. Then present a separate way that their interest or concern could be addressed independently of the topic under discussion and revisit the presented arguments and data. For example, someone worried about their job security may over-optimistically present market data or the likelihood of project success.

Chapter 9
Build Capabilities to Seize and Replicate

'Ready, Fire, Aim' ... .
... initiatives can be course corrected but opportunities are lost by delay.

TM: Strong leadership [has] a clear sense of direction. Ask, 'Will it make the boat go faster?'[79] But first [you need] to set the goal: where are they going? A leadership role is about giving voice and direction and setting the pace. What is the pace at which we should be travelling now, at this time? Pace is like the pressure you put on the team – you need to adjust it in response to the condition of the players and the circumstances and objectives you have.

Continuing with the analogy of a professional tennis player, one of their attributes is speed of action; the ability to seize the moment. What must be done now to respond to the unfolding play and turn the game to my advantage? The player must continuously move on the 'balls of their feet' and think. This concept is vitally important to competitive performance yet is often overlooked in traditional approaches to the leadership of an enterprise. Leaders need to keep the organisation in a state of anticipation for what might happen next and maintain movement, adjusting resources, teams, and initiatives in anticipation of changes that may occur, not just in response after the event. The judgement and decision making is during the game; this is not the pre-game strategy planning but responding to what unfolds in real-time. The decisions made of the 'shots' to play are within the framework of the intended strategy of how to win this match and the longer-term mission (perhaps to win the tournament). The notion of 'replicate' is like the tennis player discovering during the match that the opponent is struggling with backhand shots; they then might try to repeat winning plays to the opponent's backhand in the future.

LB: Leaders must continue to [re]act quickly to external changes brought about by the 4IR, especially if those changes exceed the anticipated pace; adaptation is increasingly important.

JH: Be extra agile as VUCA increases; you must move quickly, seizing opportunities and responding to challenges.

RB: Yes, listen more and have curiosity, but more is needed. [You also need to] have the ability to integrate different perspectives – to boil it down to 'what does this mean to us today?' – you have to act.

KC: Agile leadership – leadership that allows leaders to navigate these complex situations, to move forward even when they don't have all the data they wish they had or need – and to do so intelligently.

SG: That awareness and the interdependency of the connections and impact on people is critical. The ability to listen, bring in opinions, and assimilate everything. It's always been the case, but it has become more critical and obvious. You must make decisions and act, not just gather information and ideas.

Maintain a Sense of Urgency

Leaders must cultivate and maintain a sense of urgency – not panic, but the imperative to 'hurry up'. You may not know what your competitors are doing, how customer behaviours are changing or what disruptions will play out in the macro-environment – but in all cases, your speed is an advantage. Many years ago, I worked with the now legendary businessman Silvio Scaglia.[80] Silvio had assembled a small team of bright young consultants, which he deployed into business units across the global network of Agnelli-owned corporations. We worked hard and fast to push through changes; executives in the business units either got on the 'rollercoaster' of transformation or were left behind. Scaglia always wanted us to go faster, so much so that we were known throughout the wider corporation by a rather unflattering label implying we were like 'fast prostitutes'; widely respected and feared. The 'can do, must do, go faster' mentality resulted in successful value creation from turnarounds and growth accelerations; later serving Silvio well when he founded and rapidly grew Fastweb.

AI: Be aware of what your competition is doing – while knowing that the most dangerous competitors are those you don't know about yet – the entrepreneurs and innovators you don't yet recognise. You must be a bit paranoid; the fuel drives the innovation flywheel.

Evolution is constant; change creates new possibilities and opportunities for the organisation's and individual's growth. Successful enterprise leaders in today's context must avoid the temptation to settle as the market, competitors, and technologies constantly evolve. Before your performance results show you are falling behind, you must lean forward and evolve the operations, offerings, and business model. Inculcate an appropriate level of sense of urgency throughout the whole organisation, creating high energy to improve firm performance through innovation and rapid experimentation. Leaders should raise the cadence of key processes and projects by shortening the SPRINT (work) period between SCRUM (coordination) meetings whenever possible while supporting and requiring teams to progress with high standards. One of the business units I was overseeing at Ingersoll-Rand had fallen behind plan for four-quarters. The General Manager produced a study report, and a taskforce was established, but two more quarters passed without significant improvement. We then deployed a regional finance manager to support the team's efforts and had monthly updates, there were changes in the trajectory of the performance, but it wasn't enough. So, we created a steering committee including regional and global resources and adopted a weekly cadence of work and review. Eight weeks later we disbanded as all the goals had been achieved. My learning from that experience has since served me well; move faster. We shouldn't have waited the first four-quarters expecting the General Manager alone to resolve the issues. We should have listened more to what the issues were and then immediately formed a team with all the required resources and worked with a weekly cadence to resolve them. It's too easy as a leader to delay action and to then move too slowly. Rather, come alongside the team that is struggling, listen to them and provide support.

For the past 20 years, much attention has been given to the need to be 'customer-centric', observing behaviours and listening to customers rather than only watching and responding to competitors' actions. A part of the rationale for being customer-focused is that you see changes that might be happening more clearly and sooner than you would by waiting for a competitor to see them and implement their actions. With a similar frame of mind, in this era of rapid evolution and application of technology, it is equally important that leadership focuses directly on the evolving technologies and their applications rather than waiting for a competitor to have already demonstrated an advance before responding. Hence, adopt the mindset of leaning forward, trialling technologies, customer-centric solutions and adjusting operations – to discover what advantages can be achieved to be better prepared should it be appropriate to scale up, switch over or otherwise adapt.

PL: Speed is key. Keep things simple; keep processes lean to maintain speed.

TM: There is the myth of bad decisions, but most of the time, there is high uncertainty – so you make a decision, and then you act, and in acting, you make a good decision. Leadership requires decision and action. It could be a decision not to act – which is different to procrastination.

Innovate More: Look Further Ahead

To thrive in our increasingly complex world, companies must move beyond digitisation and reimagine what they do to create value.[81] However, most management processes are designed for leaders who have been schooled and grown their careers through conserving, protecting, and advancing existing businesses. This mindset leads to the 70–20–10 spread of spending in investment,[82] whereby approximately 70% is allocated to projects and initiatives expected to generate returns within the current planning cycle through advances to existing activities; 10% is speculative, with returns expected in a future scenario that may or may not come into existence, and the balance of 20% sit between these two. Due to financial constraints or reduced confidence in future forecasts, the investment in the speculative category is at risk of being paused to protect the investment in initiatives for the shorter term. Our research, although conducted in 2012, indicated that, even at that time, the value creation for the enterprise because of these investments was almost the exact opposite, i.e., 70% of the value increment to the enterprise would come from projects initially considered to be in the speculative 10% category. As 'the future' is approaching us at increased speed, we must look farther ahead to be ready. The 70–20–10 spending ratio on innovation projects needs to shift.

The speed of innovation to respond to changes and to influence the direction of the evolution of marketspace has even greater importance as the context of business accelerates and inherent uncertainties undermine the reliability of forecasting. To think about it another way, the duration of planning periods reduces as the change in the context in which you are operating accelerates – so we need to update and change plans more frequently. Thus, we shift our spending on innovation to more speculative projects, as the future will arrive sooner but remains unknown. As the present is less stable, the '70%' spending on innovations for this planning horizon will be relevant for a shorter period, with a reduced opportunity to deliver a return on investments. Figures don't exist for how far the investment balance in innovation projects should move, but I now look for 50–30–20 (the 20% being the most speculative).

Leaders who 'lean forward' into the unfolding future recognise that the risk of missing out or being late to market is as important a consideration as the risk of failure to achieve projected project outcomes. As noted in the *Harvard Business Review* article, 'Reinventing Your Leadership Team',[83] 'CEOs need to fundamentally rethink their leadership teams so that their top executives focus on advancing meaningful change rather than managing the current business.'

AB: The differentiating characteristics of successful leaders in this 21st century are essentially two: to be a constant innovator in business and to be highly credible within your organisation. Of course, those two characteristics have always been essential, but nowadays, the definition has changed compared to the past.

Innovation should be continuous. Technology and digitalisation are stimulating the innovation of products, services and new business models at an unprecedented rate. However, while in the past, an entrepreneur who was able to introduce a new business model or product might enjoy decades of competitive advantage, innovation has now become a daily requirement to face a frantically fast-changing environment. The leader looks into the future (evolving customer behaviours, technology applications, geopolitical shifts), and then pushes innovation every day in every area.

Address Adaptive Challenges

The phrase 'wicked problems' was introduced in 1973[84] to describe a challenge with many causes, players and interrelationships that cannot be mapped is difficult to describe and cannot be solved with traditional approaches. Then, in 2001, Heifetz and Laurie made the distinction between adaptive and technical challenges,[85] saying that adaptive ones are complex, new, have not been resolved before and are, therefore, the domain of leaders. Whereas technical challenges have been seen before and can be addressed with careful thought and analysis of data; therefore, they are the domain of managers. Complex challenges without existing solutions increasingly confront leaders as the speed of evolution of the context in which we operate accelerates, and the breadth of factors that are seemingly in motion expands. Addressing these types of challenges requires a different approach.

- The first requirement is to recognise when the challenge is 'adaptive' rather than 'technical'. Not all challenges are adaptive, and many can therefore be resolved directly. The leader must have the perspective to see across the organisation and the ability to recognise when a systemic issue involves or impacts many parties and thus requires collective attention. Managers often become frustrated in addressing adaptive challenges as the solution is out of their control; they can implement partial solutions to elements within their domain, which may cause further problems elsewhere or not address the fundamental issue. The need to respond to the disruption caused by Covid was such a situation. An enterprise-level response with activation involving multiple departments and teams was required.

- The second requirement of the leader in the face of these challenges is to maintain the collective focus on finding solutions rather than allowing various managers to focus on the parts they are each most comfortable with. The leader must ensure enterprise-level thinking and recognition of the interdependencies between managers. Whilst overseeing the collective process, the leader must be the guardian and promoter of the values and the mission of the enterprise, keeping the team focused on resolving the challenge whilst keeping sight of the purpose of the enterprise and within the guidelines of the corporate values.

- A third requirement is that the leader champions an experimenter's mindset. The solution is unknown, and the future is unknown, but actions are required. The leader must be sufficiently involved in the details and discussions of the team so that they can champion the ideas that have the most resonance and encourage and support their piloting. An experimenter's mindset seeks to launch thoughtfully but quickly, intending to learn what works and what doesn't from the experiment. It requires choosing a 'safe' place to trial and keen observation of impact and reaction in the wider system. The expectation is that what is trialled is not the final solution and may be abandoned, but the learning is valuable.

- The fourth ability of the leader in the face of these challenges is the willingness to pivot rapidly in the face of disconfirming data and insight, strenuously avoiding a culture of blame whilst seeking to maximise learning related to both the situation and how to improve the collective process in anticipation of the next adaptive challenge.

TC: Be prepared for stuff that's not understood. Be prepared for aspects of work that can't be comprehended. Don't be frightened to face it. Seek to understand. Be brave to ensure that decisions are as informed as possible in the time available – and then make a judgement call guided by your values.

Pause, Reflect and Experiment: Build Capabilities to Seize and Replicate

(1) How strong are the capabilities to seize new solutions and replicate/scale them rapidly?
- Are innovations pioneered in one market space quickly replicated in other markets?
- Do you have models that describe the expected development pathway of each market and clarity on how to compete at each evolution stage?
- How do you seek to influence the evolution of regulation and competitive dynamics in each market space, or are you reactive to changes?

(2) Prioritise and accelerate innovation.
- Ignite innovation energy with an experimenter's mindset.
- Reveal new opportunities and potential solutions to challenges at pace by applying design thinking principles, test-to-discover, rapid experimentation (ready-fire-aim) and double-loop learning.
- Keep informed about applications and new possibilities enabled by the deployment of technology; use such possibilities to fuel creative thinking.

(3) Identify and appropriately address Adaptive Challenges rather than treating them as technical challenges.
- Engage with a broad spectrum of people likely to be affected or have insights.
- Expect tension and disagreement, provide support and keep the team focused.
- Adopt an experimenter's mindset, probing, trialling actions, monitoring emergent results and then adjusting or reversing prior steps.
- Keep anchored on the superordinate goal, the purpose and the values.

(4) Invest in creating alternative scenarios and identifying potential options for actions.

(5) Plan 'future-back' rather than 'present-forward' to increase momentum and resilience.
- 'Future-back' focuses on the 'destination' (outcome), knowing that multiple alternative pathways might lead there.
- 'Present-forward' seeks to be definitive on the next step and indicative of subsequent steps on an envisioned pathway.

Chapter 10
Build Capabilities to Reposition and Reconfigure

Anchor on Purpose to increase Agility.

The third capability required for building the dynamic capacity of the enterprise is to be able to reposition and reconfigure. It is the ability to adjust, in a timely manner, the way the enterprise operates, the positioning of its offerings and its business model either incrementally or more radically. Building on the analogy of the tennis player, the first set of capabilities – 'Sense and Make Sense' – enables the player to anticipate where the ball is going and how quickly and to intuit where the opposing player may be most likely to move. The second set of capabilities – 'Seize and Replicate' – enables the tennis player to make timely decisions about what shots to play to return the ball and to make the winning play. The third set of capabilities enables the tennis player to change the dynamic of the match by strengthening their position on the court, forcing the opponent to adjust their game.

Making decisions on how to reposition and reconfigure in advance of the 'burning platform' of firm-threatening losses requires both intellectual horsepower and courage. The process must involve others to consider multiple perspectives, increase understanding of the situation, and broaden support for the actions. Group-based strategic planning processes, such as scenario planning or road mapping, can facilitate such involvement.

KC: It is critical to develop the capacity for change; individual, team, system – the ability to adapt. There is an element of speed, but only when it is required. Speed is not the most important aspect. You need to have judgement and to be consulting the right people, combining fast and slow thinking.

WN: Look for the opportunity in the changes – maybe rebuild your company: disruptive Jujitsu!

Move Ahead by Adopting a Real Options Mindset

Move ahead with options of what you might do next rather than wait on a definitive 'go/no-go' decision. The concept of a 'real option' is easy to understand and highly powerful at creating a way to move forward in otherwise impossible-to-resolve (or financially model) situations. We may not know now if a planned investment will generate the required return (above the ROI, NPV, IRR hurdles that the company uses) or if the new product or service will be successful, yet the time window for taking a decision is closing. So, rather than taking a 'leap of faith' (gamble), delaying or 'walking away', we consider what an initial first investment or action could be and what subsequent action steps it could create.

For example, we might not have the data to decide if we should open a factory in a rapidly developing market (a new country for us to enter). Still, we can see that real estate in suitable locations is increasing rapidly in price, and the available supply of land is dwindling. We may decide to buy a suitable plot of land as a first step. With the land secured, we then have options – real options. We can wait for the anticipated market development before having the confidence to build the factory, or if we want to be more cautious, we could establish a warehousing operation on the acquired land. A third option might be to sell the land if the market doesn't develop at the rate we anticipated or if unknowns such as border controls change to the point that we don't need a factory in that country.

The real options approach is very powerful in contexts of uncertainty and rapid change; it can speed up decision-making (as we do not need high confidence from, as yet, not-available data on the future). It also helps the creation of options/possibilities for how we might act as the future unfolds and enable quick implementation of subsequent steps (the options for subsequent actions having been identified in advance).

JV: When Covid happened – we were ready – as we had put in all the preparation – I didn't know it was going to happen – but I had prepared the organisation for growth – as my gut told me to do so.

CE: Be ready for the next 'Black Swan' – business/strategic/continuity planning is an important skill set – and will increase in importance. [This fosters] the skill of crisis management and preparation.

MH: You need to be highly imaginative, which the traditional model of leaders isn't. You have to prepare multiple options and quickly understand who you need help from in a different way so you make the right decisions and your decision-making process makes them look and feel legitimate.

Embrace Also-And Thinking

Many enterprises adhere to the traditional organisational approach of separating those who focus on the future from those required to deliver the results today. For example, an auto manufacturer may establish a new EV (Electric Vehicle) division whilst maintaining the core production and development focused on combustion engines and the established company brands. But, as the speed of business accelerates, and instability is the 'new normal', the separation of goals to different teams or individuals impedes adaptability and flexibility. Resources, knowledge and budgets don't readily flow between the different divisions. An alternative approach is to strive to empower the individuals and teams closest to the market to respond to the changes, thereby achieving performance results today (in the core) while also adapting (developing) for tomorrow. To do so requires the expectation and incentive for also-and thinking. Empower and enable teams to straddle the issue, for example, incorporate new technologies and approaches into the design and development of all vehicle management solutions, EV and traditional.

My work repeated demonstrates that the greater the proportion of the organisation engaged in also-and thinking, the greater the ability of the enterprise to adapt and enhance performance, particularly in dynamic, turbulent contexts. When you break down silos by integrating teams you discover new energy and hidden talent. Tushman and O'Reilly describe 'establishing a balance between optimising current firm performance (refining routines) and seeking new configurations of activities and assets for future competitive advantage.'[86] Professor Roger Martin, the former Dean of the Rotman School of Management, published his work on integrative thinking in 2007. He highlighted the differentiating impact of integrative thinking (managing with the tension of opposing objectives) for the performance of corporations and exceptional leaders: 'Successful CEO(s) ... have the predisposition and the capacity to hold in their heads two opposing ideas at once. And then, without panicking or simply settling for one alternative or the other, they're able to creatively resolve the tension between those two ideas by generating a new one that contains elements of the others but is superior to both. This process of consideration and synthesis can be termed "integrative thinking"'.[87]

It is essential not to overburden the integrated teams with the tensions they are straddling, the enterprise leader retains ownership of the most challenging paradox and helps focus the work of the integrated team.

KC: The ability to manage complexity and paradox requires a combination of intellectual horsepower (cognitive ability) and comfort with ambiguity (psychometric frameworks) – [there is often] ambiguity in the form of paradoxical situations that seem to be intractable. [These are] very complex trade-offs. You need to be smart enough to understand that the situation is complex or paradoxical. People tend to oversimplify the context.

SG: Assimilating and integrating all of these competing calls for [...] attention and not exploding or failing; it's an incredibly challenging task.

RB: Raw intelligence helps a lot with this (even if it is not fashionable to say this).

RP: A modern successful leader needs to be able to deal with ambiguity in a more immediate and pressing way than at any other time in recent history. What little certainty there was in predicting the future from the activities of the past has become a distant memory in our immediate post-pandemic world. More than ever, leaders have to own, translate and deal with ambiguity and complexities in every part of their business. [...] The world of leadership has fundamentally changed, and the modern successful leader needs to be a more rounded, complete and 'ambidextrous' individual than ever before.

Drive Productivity With Technology

Labour productivity statistics abound, comparing sectors, job types, age groups and countries. However, what matters most is the productivity that you achieve in your enterprise. Strangely, when the subject of productivity is brought up, there is often a sense of discomfort; a look crosses people's faces as if they are thinking about cost-cutting and redundancies and worried whether this means that the enterprise is struggling. Sadly, such reactions do not reflect the positivity that should come from seeking to extend the value-add of people as the tasks they do and how they do them inevitably change. Making the jobs that people do more centred on human skills whilst offloading other tasks to technology can be empowering and more satisfying for the worker, as well as raising the level of productivity. For example, the Chief People Officer at a major global company recently shared that 40 of her 100 staff were now using generative AI daily. This move has not resulted in a reduction in headcount, but in increased time these HR officers spend speaking with people, the executives and staff they are tasked to support.

Three broad approaches to raising productivity are:

(a)   Seek to produce higher value-added products and services with the same scale of workforce. A much-discussed example is that you could be trading the commodity of coffee, or you could create a branded version of coffee (such as Nescafé), or you could open a café or coffee shop and sell cups of coffee – or you could seek to create a Starbucks-type coffee chain – where you are selling an experience rather than focusing on the quality of the coffee being sold. An alternative strategy might see you focus on the higher value-added offerings within the overall portfolio – such as seeking to sell more SUVs rather than compact cars.

(b)   Seek to produce more volume, with the same scale of workforce – or the same output volume with fewer workers. This was very much the logic that drove the growth of mass production and automation during the 2nd and 3rd Industrial Revolutions. The role of technology in enabling such productivity gains is often ignored in union and media commentary, which instead promotes the assumption that if there are fewer workers, those that remain must work harder to 'cover' for the colleagues that are no longer there.

(c)   Seek to redesign work so that humans do what humans do best (creative tasks, solving problems, being highly adaptive), and automation does what automation does best (repetitive tasks, accessing and processing huge amounts of data, working dangerous [to humans] conditions). The 4th Industrial Revolution (4IR) is enabling a huge shift in what work humans do.

It is this third approach that particularly sets the productivity performance of enterprises apart from each other. The strategy adopted will be specific to each enterprise; however, increasingly, leaders see the opportunity to raise their organisation's productivity by embracing the technologies and approaches of the 4th Industrial Revolution.

AI: For example, consider productivity – central and regional governments don't have expertise in productivity, and therefore, we shouldn't look to them to solve the problem – rather, businesses need to step up and fix the problem for themselves and with each other. There is too much jumping to national solutions and initiatives. Instead, it should be up to the government to set a mission for the country, and then businesses and other sector players take up the challenge. The HR profession is a major inhibitor of productivity growth by defining job 'boxes' and metrics and rewards systems that they then force on their organisation. We need to refocus to measure performance on output; the current bias is to measure inputs. We need to get a better alignment of activities to the goals of the enterprise – way too much time is spent doing things that are not exactly aligned with the outcomes we seek to achieve. I would say that HR is one of the biggest reasons for low productivity in the UK; they need to accelerate the switch to an output-based orientation.

BJ: [Our] UK law firm needed to get a document done, requiring them to work over the weekend – a junior lawyer said, 'I'm not doing it as I've got a rock concert to go to' … Now, what do you do? Compare this to our Chinese client – who works 9 AM to midnight, seven days a week – with a 90-minute subway ride each way – and takes one week off per year. This is normal in China. It means that each Chinese person works twice as hard as a UK worker. The Chinese lawyer is likely to have attended the same law school as the UK lawyer (and maybe even graduated with higher grades). If the UK firm is going to survive, it must find ways of raising its productivity; now, as they are not in China, they won't have Chinese working practices – so they need to find ways to work smarter.

WS: The UK is a welfare, dare I say 'Nanny', state – where the benefits are so good that a significant proportion of the labour force does not want to work. Of course, there are constant complaints in the media about benefits not keeping up with inflation and underfunding of the NHS [National Health Service], etc. Still, the fact is that the UK is a high-tax nation with high benefits, a large proportion of the labour force that is 'non-productive', and economic growth that has 'flat-lined'. As the media and unions keep demanding more hand-outs and state funding and each government refuses to change course, the national economy can only grow if individual businesses drive increases in their productivity.

PC: Productivity, output for labour hours input is a major problem for the UK. The UK has a high proportion of low-skilled jobs – higher than most developed countries because of systematic underinvestment in technology. This has been partly allowed to happen as we have had a liberal labour market, which was allowed to persist due to migrant labour from Europe. [...] Brexit is perhaps helping, as it has removed the large pool of lower-cost labour, so now managers are having to think about reimagining work, both to raise productivity and attract back into the workforce those who have opted to be disengaged economically.

BS: A big issue is the labour shortage – a small percentage of the population wants to work. The productivity growth rate has been anaemic for decades. Therefore, we have to look at automation – we are trialling solutions. This is a good thing. It is often for dirty jobs that used to be done by foreign labour – so Brexit has changed things – which may be a positive, but right now, it's a difficult time.

Pause, Reflect and Experiment: Build Capabilities to Reposition and Reconfigure

(1) How strong are the capabilities to think differently, challenge boundaries and compete differently?

(2) How much attention and investment has been put into making the enterprise digitally fit for the future?
- Has there been a significant, concerted programme to transform productivity by leveraging technologies?
- Have digital tools, analytics and collaborative platforms been adopted throughout the enterprise, transforming employee, customer, operations, supply chain management and leadership activities?

(3) What is the attitude to change? Is it thought of as painful and episodic or energising and continuous?

(4) Are you defining new marketspaces or adopting established sector norms?
- Do you work collaboratively with other companies to change competitive dynamics and the sources of competitive advantage you leverage?

(5) Practice Also-And thinking. Look for more options and alternatives when faced with either/or situations or a compromise between competing requests or objectives. For example, either the customer service or manufacturing department can get the extra headcount they request, or you could think about a half-head count for each. A better approach might be to see if the problems they are each looking to solve with the extra headcount could be resolved in another way. Is there a dependency between the two? For example, is extra customer service required because of manufacturing errors?

- Stop and pause when facing opportunities and challenges; think about how to question the ongoing relevance of existing paradigms and perspectives. Are assumed trade-offs, competitor behaviours, and resource constraints still relevant?
- Frame the key questions and boundaries rather than seeking problem definition and solution.
- Look for opportunities to adopt a 'Also-And' mindset, challenging existing/ legacy assumptions.

Chapter 11
Flow: Increase the Mobility of Resources

Hire for fit. Train for skills. Deploy for impact.

RW: Our new organisation model is where we try to distance ourselves from the assumption that technical leaders should become senior leaders – we are breaking free from the idea that technical leaders must also become experts as people leaders. In the future, perhaps we need to move towards a situation where we have both a technical leader AND a people leader – two different people – both being paid for seniority. Perhaps this is my old communist upbringing – where we had a 'political' leader and an 'organisational' leader – they had to co-exist in every situation. However, I do think that the idea that someone gets promoted to be a people leader after years of demonstrating their technical capabilities is beyond stupid. Why does it have to be a skilled surgeon to run a hospital? Why do you need a highly published research academic to run a university? Technical skills do not give you managerial skills or leadership skills.

Fluid Organisation

One of the greatest challenges in today's context is ensuring that the best, most relevant talent (which is in short supply) is deployed against the most important and urgent initiatives. It is especially difficult as those initiatives compete for attention while circumstances continuously change. The solution is to be able to fluidly deploy and redeploy people from across the enterprise to anywhere throughout the enterprise, while training and developing more! However, such an enterprise-wide approach contrasts with the traditional view of the organisation, which defines functions, specialisation and departments and identifies people not for the skills that they have but the job 'box' they are in. Chapter 7 explored the importance of treating teams as the enterprise's 'engines' of performance and how leadership is increasingly viewed as a 'team' activity. Adopting such approaches across the enterprise represents a significant shift from traditional human resource management practices and thinking. It necessitates adopting new mindsets, cultures and processes.

For most of the 20th century and the early part of the 21st century, human resource managers' core approach has been deciding for the employees what they should be doing and how they should be doing it; deciding which people merit being trained and developed, when and how. The approach has been to fit people with an infinite variety of skills, circumstances, strengths, weaknesses, motivations, and conflicting obligations into standard 'boxes' called job descriptions and the audacity to expect everyone to behave in the prescribed way. This system is unsuitable for supporting the resource-fluid, talent-centric enterprise we need today. Generations of human resource managers should be held to account for the dehumanisation of the working experience and being key contributors to what the World Health Organisation calls the 'epidemic of stress'. One of the greatest changes required in the 4th Industrial Revolution is to become talent-centric, providing an environment where people can be the best version of themselves, whatever that may be. Fully 82% of the companies surveyed say that their approaches to human resources management are currently one of control and risk mitigation. Yet there is also hope, as a 2020 report by McKinsey and Company[88] found that 70% of respondents are keen to adopt agile teaming practices.

SB1: [There is a] need to think enterprise-wide now – not being parochial: what's best for the enterprise – not your department? The shocks that we must respond to require an enterprise-wide mindset. Successful leadership should be doing this on a day-to-day basis, not just in crises. Performance metrics are so messed up – HR has had the wrong mandate for far too long. You do not get the best results for the enterprise by defining metrics and reward systems for the performance of siloes. If I had my way, I would fire the whole HR leadership team and bring in people who actually think that talent matters, that talent needs to be deployed to the most important and pressing issues, and that talent needs to be financially rewarded in ways that align with their contribution on each specific issue.

Home and Away Teams

The concept of 'home' and 'away' teams is a step away from siloed, department thinking and towards fluid teaming. The 'home' team is a functional, department or business unit team where the individual resides when not part of a cross-functional team. In the 'home team', there is clarity of who is the line manager, a job-description 'box', a pay-grade band and a performance review cycle. HR is comfortable with these trappings. However, in addition, the individual joins 'away' teams to work on projects with others that are brought from other departments or functions. The greater the proportion of time that the individual spends in the 'away' team, the greater the emphasis on assessing and rewarding their contribution in the 'away' team, and the lower the emphasis placed on the 'home team'. The extension of the concept is one where the individual's performance, compensation and progression are all determined by their contribution to 'away' teams.

Talent/Project Marketplace

Technology provides significant help when it comes to managing a fluid organisation. For starters, there needs to be a marketplace that matches upcoming projects requiring sets of skills with individuals, from wherever in the corporation, with their own combinations of skills. An individual's skills or competence level are not defined by the job 'box' that HR recognises. As such it is essential that the language of the talent/project marketplace is skills and competency levels not job description or pay grade. The performance of the individuals during the team assignment needs to be tracked so that relevant feedback can be provided, and records kept of the value-add and progression of each individual. Feedback, reviews and development training need to be conducted or available at the rhythm of the projects, not constrained by periodic cycles.

The more effective and skilled your organisation is at deploying and managing teams, the more comfortable you must be with rebuilding or disbanding them. Reconstituting teams and recycling team members is essential and to be expected. Organisational needs and priorities change, team mandates, contexts, individual circumstances, energy levels, learnings, and skills evolve. The team members who have performed well in getting to a certain point, pioneering the way, may not be the members most suited for continuing to take the initiative forward to the next level. As a leader, you must be looking forward and preparing the team that needs to exist next. Don't wait, as the market and competition will not wait for you. Rule 2 of Sir Alex Ferguson's 10-point formula for successful teams is 'dare to rebuild your team'. It's important to note that this is not Rule 10. It's not an afterthought. Keeping the team membership fresh requires active attention and the courage not to leave an existing successful line-up undisturbed for too long. As noted in the *HBR* article, 'Ferguson's Formula',[89] Even in times of great success, Ferguson worked to rebuild his team. 'He's never really looking at this moment, he's always looking into the future,' said one of the players, 'Knowing what needs strengthening and what needs refreshing – he's got that knack.' The leader sets the tone for this mobility (within the organisation). Mobility is in service of overall performance. Mobility creates an on-going set of opportunities for individual talent to be discovered and develop further. Mobility reduces the impact of the bias of managers for an individual's career, pay and progression. Mobility provides the opportunity and incentive for individuals to continue to upskill and reskill.

DH: Don't hold on to the winning team of players too long – rebuild before the weakness shows. Ensure consistent performance.

SGJ: The team is only as strong as the weakest person. Three weak links will be more poisonous than 25 great aligned folks. It needs to be BOTH the performance in the game AND how everyone comes together as a team – the team experience, off the court. Unfortunately, in the X-Championship, we underperformed – the team experience was great, but not the results – not the individual accountability on the court.

New Concepts of Organisation

A new dominant model of organisation has yet to emerge, but what is evident is that more agility is required than can be provided by traditional forms (such as departmental, matrix or hub and spoke). Network models and the 'team of teams'[90] approach provide greater resource mobility and structural flexibility. The success of the 'team of teams' approach depends on having a strong unifying sense of purpose, a commonly shared doctrine for how to come together, and the willingness to pool resources and information. Equally there should be the expectancy to engage external resources (security requirements permitting), to provide changes in capacity and to access specialist skills. In his book *Reinventing Organisations*,[91] Frederic Laloux describes the 'teal' type of organisation as one where people flow to teams where they are most needed, the teams are self-managing, authority is distributed throughout the network and natural hierarchies emerge and disperse. I urge HR officers to see each individual in the enterprise as a valuable, unique, and multi-skilled person. That staff are engaged by the enterprise independent of any specific role or position, department, or function. That individuals are then dynamically matched to project and needs whilst all the time being supported, encouraged, and rewarded for upskilling and reskilling.

ML: In organisations with a high density of talent [lots of similar talent, e.g., a professional services firm], you need to facilitate more fluid movement. Do we need to have a pyramid structure? Does the leader need to be at the top? Who is the worker of the future? It's increasingly helpful to think of workers as semi-autonomous contractors rather than locked-in employees, and as location matters less, we have the concept of the disaggregated enterprise. Leaders have less grip on the workers; they come and go as they see best to fit their needs.

JA: The workforce that leaders are asked to mobilise may be dispersed and unaffiliated to a specific individual leader. And it may be comprised of local, regional, global and automated (AI/ML) entities. The way that the division of labour and optimisation of the function of such teams occurs will be the biggest challenge for the future leader.

MH: [It is critical] to bring people together and have them collaborate. Connect people across your networks and connect networks – this is increasingly the role of leaders.

JA: Covid has forced us to reimagine the office, and what it means in a world where our workforce can function remotely, and hybrid organisations are not only possible but desirable for many of our best and brightest. The office may not be the place you work, but the place where you provide common spaces for bounce and build innovation, receive upskilling and training to broaden your technical and leadership capabilities and form a community through providing spaces and services generally not associated with the office building of today.

CU: An understanding of human energy is increasingly important ... engagement, relationships/social ties at work, meaningful work ... those who have close friends at work are 10% more engaged and productive. Whereas people are feeling less and less connected at work. Therefore, leaders need to be experts at constantly making connections themselves and connecting people with others in the workplace. We have to make interest in other humans almost an explicit activity.

Enterprise Thinking: All of One Company

One of the most important shifts required to achieve mobility in human resources is the sense of all being of one big team, sometimes called 'enterprise-wide thinking'. How many times have you made (or have you heard about) a well-intentioned request for additional resources only to be told 'no' or offered a more junior (i.e., cheaper) alternative? The accompanying narrative may be that there is only so much budget, and the headcount has been allocated to a different department.

This model of management by controlling resource allocation fractures the enterprise, reinforcing the notion of 'my' resources vs. 'your' resources, 'my objectives' being in tension with 'your objectives'. A fluid organisation, where talent from whichever department can join a team addressing a priority issue for the enterprise, necessitates that department heads, supervisors and individual contributors identify themselves as belonging to the same big team; 'all of one company'. As a CEO in one corporation, I became so fed up with the silo mentality and whining about the resources needed to achieve objectives from department heads that in one meeting I 'told' (not very gently!) all assembled that everyone worked for me, so if the department heads couldn't collaborate then I would return all of them to being team members and assign them and everyone else to interdepartmental teams myself. I don't recommend such an outburst – but the point is made. Everyone's success depends on the enterprise's success, if department or business unit goals and resources are an obstacle to that success, then change the mindset, structure and processes. We are all of one team, one company.

PM: 'All of one company' … we are obsessed with division and individualism – we need to focus on the fact that, with all our differences, we are all in it together. What are your strengths? Are you good enough for what we are trying to do – are you right for the job? We will have disagreements, but we are working together for one purpose. Give credit to whichever person has provided input, even if you disagree or take an alternative course of action – recognise their contribution. We must come together. All of one company, all in it together.

SB: Enterprise thinking – more shocks will come – enterprise thinking increases adaptability. You might have to reduce staff or, restructure or take on a difficult project that others have shunned. Avoid sclerosis that results from territorial/department-level thinking. It's not your resource – we all work for the same enterprise.

TM: Leadership is about uniting the team/the whole organisation to be greater than the sum of the parts.

Establishing the sense of 'one company' requires everyone to feel a sense of belonging and to identify with the enterprise's objectives, purpose and values. The head of Engineering at a lossmaking major airline which was struggling to be turned around, was little moved by the frustrations of the head of Cabin

Services, who was reporting unhappy passengers. Engineering had achieved the targeted cost savings; it had been painful, but it was done. He thought Cabin Services needed to 'hold the line' and achieve theirs too. Except that, having pushed through the required cuts in Cabin Service, unhappy passengers were now resulting in bad press and plummeting revenues. There wouldn't be any airline left if some services weren't restored in the cabin – which would mean looking to other areas, like Engineering, for further savings. Adopting the mindset of 'all of one company' rather than siloed thinking enabled the heads of Engineering, Ground Services and Cabin Services to work together to find ways to benefit the airline, the whole enterprise, not just their department.

Fluid Enterprises

Conduct an orchestra of virtuosos, don't build a 'well-oiled machine'

Resources (talent, digital, knowledge, physical) will increasingly be shared (or rented) rather than owned. This behaviour is already evident in the use of 'gig economy' freelancers, the migration to shared usage of cloud capacity and applications, and the use of shared offices and meeting spaces rather than dedicated corporate facilities.

DH: The younger generations have a good awareness of what they do and what others can do. They are very comfortable in projects – rather than linear careers. They are much less likely to be generalists. There is momentum to choose to be a specialist, work independently, and create your own life/work balance. They accept that neither the public social care system nor a company will pay for their pension or healthcare.

JA: The workforce that leaders mobilise may be dispersed and unaffiliated to a specific organisation; it may comprise local, regional, global and automated (AI/ML) entities. How the division of labour and optimisation of the function of such teams occurs will be the biggest challenge for the future leader.

ML: We are changing now to a [population] of contractors rather than employees. – the disaggregated enterprise. A leader has less grip on the employees; they come and go as they see best fits their needs. If we can move to a high talent density model – where talent leverages AI and ML [machine learning], you can facilitate more fluid movement of people. Do we need to have a pyramid structure? Does the leader need to be at the top? Surely, the leader needs to be more in the centre, coordinating and connecting resources and projects. In the future, I think we have to question the value of managers. Contractors can self-manage – increasingly, we treat employees as self-managing and are comfortable contracting with external contractors. So we might start reducing the levels of managers in an organisation. How do they add value if people can self-manage and if we increasingly assemble teams to tackle projects?

Pause, Reflect and Experiment: Flow, Increase the Mobility of Resources

(1) Do you have the right mix of skills to transform for and thrive in the 4th Industrial Revolution?
- Are you effective at recruiting talent with future relevant skills?
- Are you able to retain talent with future relevant skills?
- Are you upskilling and reskilling workers at pace to ensure future relevance?

(2) Are you redesigning jobs to focus people on higher value-added activities, embracing generative AI (and other technologies) to improve efficiency?

(3) How empowered and fluid are your human resources?
- Do people move across and through the organisation? Can you ensure your talent is deployed smoothly to the most important tasks and redeployed as priorities change?
- Is there a strong sense of belonging to 'one team' across the enterprise?
- Are individuals empowered? Do they have the expectation and responsibility to enhance performance?

(4) Create a skills-based project/talent marketplace.
- Update and unify skills definitions across the company; define the skills requirements of all jobs.
- Encourage employees to review and share their skill sets, whether used or not in their current role.
- Define projects around business priorities – specify multi-functional teams and skill sets required to address the project.
- Enable talent/project matching through skill sets.

- Track, recognise and reward team-based contributions of individuals. Provide timely and constructive feedback to individuals for their performance in project teams and the development or application of their skills.
- Encourage and support staff to self-direct their skills development.

(5) Create the culture of 'all of one company'.
- Do you consider your enterprise to consist of departments and business units or as 'one team' made up of many smaller teams that fluidly assemble, perform, and then renew?
- Role model 'all of one company' (enterprise thinking) in the top team.
- Cascade these skills and culture through the managers and supervisors to all employees.
- Look out for stand-out talent, support and develop them with stretch deployments to priority projects and, if required, individual employment terms (I-deals).

PART FIVE
Accelerate

Time is short, and your energies are finite; learn faster. 'Accelerate' emphasises increasing the pace of progress, while 'continuous' communicates the need for on-going, consistent development; both are important mindsets for leaders today.

Chapter 12
Be the Best You

If you can't lead yourself, why should you lead others?

Aspiration Drives Self-development

Why do we strive to become better? Why do others invest in our development? Because there is an impact that we want to achieve – a mission, purpose, or vision that we have and that, maybe, others believe in. If others voluntarily invest in your development, you are already a leader. You have responsibility to be the best you can be and achieve the impact that you have been imagining. The greater this 'calling', the more challenges we must overcome, and the greater the leadership prowess that we need to achieve. If we want to run a marathon but it's been years since we completed even a 5k, then we will need to know the time until the anticipated race, seek out a training and diet plan, buy the right clothes and start the training – and then continue with self-discipline and self-control. If we are lucky, we might also have a coach, trainer, or mentor; but none of these matter if we don't have the vision and the discipline. The more passionate we are about the goal, the more rigorously we will stick with the training and the diet. We might be supported by running companions who run with us, sharing advice and encouragement. But if we continually slip off the plan, cheat on the diet and skip our sessions with our coach, it's unlikely we will complete the marathon. Moreover, our running companions will be less inclined to book their time to join us as we might cancel future sessions, which would undermine their training for the race.

The following section introduces the elements of self-leadership that I have found to be most effective. However, I don't believe there is one single formula; instead, you must assemble the elements that work for you – and hold them together with persistence. Growth as a leader should be a continuous process without an end. Also, the journey of growing as a leader is not linear; there will be slip-ups, mistakes, failures, and successes – DO NOT let any of these derail you.

Hold Tightly to Your Vision of Your Future Self

One of the most frequent themes when speaking with already successful leaders is their acknowledgement of their commitment to continuously improving themselves: learning about new challenges, opportunities and possibilities while also monitoring their performance and energies against the high standards they hold for themselves. It takes this self-discipline and hard work to be the best version of themselves all the time while also pushing themselves to be better for tomorrow.

Write down your contract with yourself; what is your goal, what will it look and feel like when you achieve it, and why does it matter to you? A useful practice for cementing commitment to the pursuit of the change desired is visualisation. Sometimes called 'functional imagery', it is described as a mental rehearsal of attaining the desired goal. It has been shown to significantly increase the likelihood of goal attainment, particularly in sports and weight loss.[92] A version of this practice is to create a collage of images on a large board (or on a computer) – a vision board. The images represent the 'what' you want to achieve and the emotion and new possibilities that achieving the outcome could create. For example, suppose the goal portrayed is an ethnic minority elite sportsman leading a team to victory in an international tournament. In that case, the imagery might include the celebration, receiving congratulations from their 'hero' as well as inspiring inner-city ethnic minority children to take up the sport.

AJ: See where you want to get to, then you can work at it.

BJ: Where do you want to be in 10 years? What does good look like [in terms of job and work-life]? Then you have to manage to that goal.

OL: Why do you want to get better – why does it matter to you? Then what will you do to work at it? Think about it. What are you doing? Who is giving you feedback? Who is holding you to account? When did you last mess up? Why? What did you learn? [This is] self-analysis. Look straight in the mirror and discipline yourself to attain the goal that you are trying to achieve.

DH: There are two types of people – those waiting for the situation to end when 'things will go back to normal' vs those managing in the new reality; they are pushing to be better given the changes that have happened and are happening. This is the difference between managers and leaders.

Know the 'Big Why' Why do you want to improve your impact as a leader? Why do you want to develop the leadership prowess you envision? Knowing the 'Big Why' for some individuals is easy; perhaps there is an immediate threat or opportunity, and you need to step up – perhaps you've been made redundant and have had a smouldering concept for a start-up for several years. You must act now before the severance pay runs out! For most, knowing the 'Big Why' is much harder as it requires stripping back the nice sounding, politically correct, safe answers that we more readily share with others and tell ourselves.

Once you know the 'Big Why', you can assess the difference between how you are now and how you need to be. Without the 'Big Why', it's hard to know what aspects of leadership you need to strengthen – it can seem rather generic and theoretical. What are the gaps between who and how you are now and how you need to be to achieve impact on the mission that you have identified? How large are those gaps? Are you looking to make incremental improvements, to 'sandpaper away' a few rough edges – or to make big strides? You may not know this – as you don't know the future challenges you will face – but it's important to reflect and seek to identify, given what you know now, the biggest areas where you feel you need to improve for the mission that you are called to.

The 'Big Why' is described by author Andrew Bryant[93] as 'intention'. He says intention is 'an inner narrative about why achieving an objective is important. Intention is the drive to be a better version of oneself and make the world a better place. Intentional action is like a laser, while unintentional action is like hitting everything with a hammer.'

Daily Discipline and Hard Work

Personal growth only happens through focused effort and discipline each day. As the author John Maxwell noted,[94] *'The secret of success is determined by your daily agenda.'* Personally I really struggle with this. In the morning I've got great intention to live healthily and exercise during the day and I know that I will complete my journal in the evening. But by 5PM I'm hungry, I have a dinner with clients looming and my day has been pretty good so far, I even ran my 5K faster than last week – and so a glass of wine is hard to resist!

OL: I have an appetite to improve myself. Every day is a learning day. [There is a] need for gradual, day-to-day discipline to improve yourself. Leadership is daily training; it is not a natural growth. Leadership development is hard work on yourself.

CU: The first component is discipline. You must be able to do something, not because you want to but because of discipline – it has to be done, not because you want to or like to. [By contrast], HR dislikes the word discipline. If you don't have self-discipline, you have nothing.

BH: One of my things was the need to win all the time – I had to reprogram myself through daily discipline and holding myself to account.

Some reliably effective techniques are described below, but you can also find others. Choose one or two and then reflect on the progress you are making. Many people make a habit of one technique but experiment with others; you have to find the formula that works best for you.

i.   Break the big goal or vision into manageable milestones through planning and goal setting. (Note: A great motivational speech on this topic is Arnold Schwarzenegger's graduation speech in 2020 amid the COVID-19 pandemic, in which he speaks about his recent heart surgery and recovery).[95] Build your confidence by creating a track record of success, starting with more easily achievable goals, milestones or other aspects of your life or leadership. These should be easier at first and then more of a stretch, faster to achieve at the beginning, then longer as you move on. Celebrate as each step is achieved. Commit to not slipping backwards.

ii.   Track progress: How will you measure your improvements? To use the weight loss analogy, what you track should be linked to the 'Big Why'. Perhaps the 'Big Why' is to reduce the risk of heart attack. 'How' you measure it could be the kilograms you lose or body fat percentage. Whereas, if your 'Big Why' was linked to health and fitness, you might track kilograms of weight loss and time spent exercising. If your 'Big Why' were to reduce the environmental impact of the automotive industry, you might track the number of electric vehicles you sell or the number you sell as a percentage of the total market.

iii. Keep a log or journal that you complete at the same time each day. Include some reflection in the journal, not just the events. For example: 'Today did I do my best to … [step towards my goal]?' or 'What did I learn today about myself and my journey?'

iv.   Combine 'sweet and sour' to build positive habits, adjusting actions to achieve your goals so that they are more appealing. This can be as simple as reframing, for instance, seeing the hard work now as a step towards your much-desired goal, e.g., a day of strict dieting as you focus on bringing your weight-loss goal closer. Alternatively, you might be committed to getting fit but prefer to watch your favourite movie, so instead, you decide to use a cross-trainer in the gym while watching your movies on a tablet.

v.   Design the change programme that best matches your balance of self-discipline or self-control. For example, I am much better at self-discipline than self-control. Put me in a pub with friends, and I am likely to order beer and chips rather than salad and sparkling water - lack of self-control. But I have the discipline to go to bed early and turn down my friends' invitation to go to the pub again, with the promise to myself that I will get up early and exercise. My lower self-control means that if meetings are running long and conversations seem circular (to me), then I know that I will feel frustrated and will probably step in, get a decision made and move on, even though I know that risks alienating some folks and may stymy the collaborative culture that I am trying to foster. However, with my better self-discipline, I know that I can adhere to laying out the structure at the start of the meeting, reiterating the doctrine of how we come together to discuss and make decisions and emphasise that I will be leaving the session at the appointed end time, though others are welcome to continue to stay and continue to debate. Knowing yourself and whether you are better at self-control or self-discipline is important, then design the change programme that matches your strengths.

vi.   Avoid 'all-or-nothing' thinking – forgive yourself when you slip up. When striving for change or growth, and you slip back into old ways or mess up a situation, you mustn't give up on yourself and your self-belief. Look at the progress that you have made to date and review your log. Pick up again. Similarly, when it's going well, don't think you've cracked it; instead, stay vigilant and keep reminding yourself of the 'Big Why'. Have self-compassion for yourself. Remember that you are seeking progress, not perfection.

vii.   Manage your fatigue. It is hard to maintain self-control or self-discipline when we are tired. What biorhythm will work best for you? For me, it is mornings; I prefer to respond to the most important e-mails and host meetings on the most complex issues in the morning. Afternoons and evenings (for me) are better spent with staff or clients, building and reinforcing relationships.

Pause, Reflect and Experiment: Be the Best You

(1) Envision the future you.
- Add texture and details to the image to make it personal and linked to your passion and purpose.
- Write yourself a letter from the future. Envision the best version of yourself, having achieved your stated goals; what would you say to the present you? What words of advice, encouragement, duty, or coercion would you give to yourself that will sustain you in developing from where/who you are now to the future you?

(2) Know the 'Big Why?' Why does it really matter to you to achieve the vision?
- What's the 'Big Why'? Your root psychological foundation, which you may uncover if you repeat this self-questioning (' ... and why does that matter to me') process until you can get to no deeper definition of 'why'.

(3) What is your manifesto, your statement of intent for the impact you will achieve and how you will achieve it? What is the reason that others should join, support, or follow you?
- Are you willing to take ownership of the journey and discipline of becoming a more responsible leader, achieving greater impact?
- Only you are responsible for the outcomes that will be achieved; no one else, and there are no mitigating circumstances.
- Make your goals explicit, write them down and read them out aloud.

Chapter 13
Bring Others With You

The shadow you cast defines the culture as lived by others.

Trust and Psychological Safety

Trust has long been recognised as essential for the success of teams and organisations. However, my work with leaders highlights an increased recognition that, in the context of high turbulence and change and the increased prevalence of virtual communities and collaboration, trust is experienced differently while still a great differentiator of performance. Performance-enabling trust today is strongly associated with four attributes:

(1)   Psychological safety – contributing and challenging thoughts, ideas, and perspectives without judging or being judged. *Trust that enables inclusion and belonging*.

(2)   Responsibility – leaders must be perceived to represent the interests of the relevant stakeholder groups. In virtual and *hybrid contexts, there must be no bias to favour or over-represent those more visible or communicative stakeholders*.

(3)   Confidence in the future – that the enterprise has a future despite the turbulence; that the staff are valued and equipped to have a positive future with the enterprise.

(4)   Equally, the leader needs to demonstrate that they trust the followers (e.g. employees or contractors) irrespective of the proximity or ease of interaction; the leader must act deliberately to demonstrate even-handedness in trusting, delegating and empowering others.

NH: Employees and collaborators have to trust you as a leader. The root of trust (which is so important) is the belief that you have their back and will do the right thing for them.

AI: [There is a] need for real collaboration within your team and confidence that your team has high personal responsibility. We also learnt this through the pandemic. Hybrid is here to stay. People will work when they need/want to – and where they want to. Therefore, leaders need to be confident in team members' responsibility to get the stuff done and deliver the outcomes. Moving away from monitoring inputs is a big shift for managers and HR. Time is no longer a proxy for the quality of work being done.

SB: The world is not easy; it's increasingly transactional, but as a leader, you need to invest in people and support their growth. The longer someone is in an organisation, the more trust and credibility they have – which means they have bigger roles and tasks and are more likely to be supported in the projects you initiate. This is trust. Trust is in short supply in the transactional context, so you stand out from others by nurturing trust.

DL: If you can establish trust, be trusted, and be known as trustworthy, then you gather others to you and trust leads to empowerment. In today's cyber context, there are those in your environment who are working deliberately against you to undermine you, but you don't know who they are. Whereas in the physical world, things were a lot clearer, in the virtual world, it is much harder. We often can't readily differentiate between what is true and what is false. In this grey world, you stand out if you are trustworthy and trusting. Then, the best will come to you as an employer, and the best opportunities will come to you as a worker. Leaders need to master the management of trust, both to be trusted and to trust and empower others without being overly exposed to or naïve about the dangers.

Delegate and Empower More

In today's context we need to increase our comfort and ability to delegate and empower others across a range of knowledge and skills areas that we ourselves do not fully understand. It is one thing to delegate, when we are confident that we can 'step in' and save the situation should there be a problem, when we are able to watch for indicators that problems might be emerging based on our own hard-won experiences, it requires greater leadership skill to do so when we do not have subject or process knowledge ourselves. Most leaders blur the definitions of delegation and empowerment. It is worth making note of the differences, as there is then the opportunity for the leader to choose how to assign tasks to others. When delegating, the leader has established the parameters of the task or challenge and assigns responsibility for finding a solution or implementing the appropriate actions to someone else. Empowerment is when the team or individual can determine for themselves the parameters of the mission, with alignment on the enterprise's overall objectives. The thought leader, John Maxwell, notes, 'One of the best ways to exert leadership influence over others is to make them feel empowered. [Move from] committees to teams of members who work together to achieve some small part of the [...] firm's mission, delegating authority to others and empowering them to take meaningful action to further a common mission is crucial.'[96] In today's context the leader must establish the environment for, ensure the healthy functioning of the team (Chapter 7) and individuals (Chapter 8) and provide the support that enables success. You must make clear, for yourself and for the individuals involved, whether you are delegating to them or empowering them, making your choice dependent on the situation, then managing the process accordingly.

JH: Empower people to make decisions vs. control all decisions.

MH: Let go – delegate to your team until you are uncomfortable – and then delegate some more. In doing so, they will rise to the opportunity. 'Fail fast, fail early'. Trust your people.

PC: Use power to distribute it to others – make others feel they can challenge me, the leader.

RP: Empower others to bring their whole selves to work while being talent catalysts for their current and future teams.

You need to delegate so that you can focus your energies on the biggest, most complex tasks facing the enterprise. You don't have the bandwidth to do everything, and it may be tempting for you to stay with the issues and domains that you know best; however, doing so will stunt your growth and that of the enterprise and will demotivate others assigned to those areas.

WS: Delegation is so important. The business will only grow if you can delegate – [the absence of] this cripples leaders and cripples growth. One of my biggest discussions with managers is their need to delegate more – and how to do it.

IS: Senior management must deal with complex problems – if they are not complex, someone more junior should address them. Leaders need to be on the detail but not tied up in the detail – but you must be able to get down into the detail; you MUST be on top of stuff.

BS: The ability to balance the strategy and the details – you need both – but you move from one to the other. Bypass senior and middle managers sometimes to see what's happening on the shop floor – so you need to know how to do this – and without offending those in between.

AI: Being able to step away from the operations – yet the organisation can make all the decisions needed to keep going. Measure your success through your absence! Leaders set guardrails – set them narrow or wide – I aim to set them wide – so absolutely there are dangers if they go beyond the rails but lots of discretion/empowerment within them.

Delegating can be hard for a new leader, but it gets easier with practice! New leaders tend to want to oversee the work of others, quality control and ensure alignment with other teams and workstreams so they are most comfortable when they make important decisions. Such behaviours are driven by their desire to fulfil their responsibility for the functioning of the areas they lead, intermingled with concern for how much they can trust the performance of the team and resources they coordinate. The leader needs to recognise that their duty is to focus on the most complex, ambiguous questions while building the capabilities of colleagues to address others. Building confidence that you can delegate tasks and empower others takes time but is accelerated by stepping beyond your comfort zone and delegating more sooner. The leader retains responsibility for the outcomes of the team or individual delegated to; therefore, be positive, even when there are setbacks, set the conditions for the team to succeed, act like a coach and be supportive.[97] Also, seek feedback from the team on how they feel you can improve your skills in delegating and empowering. After all, your goals are to build up the team's (or individuals') capabilities so that you can delegate more to them and become more effective at delegating and empowering.

PC: Galvanise the resources around you to reach the best possible outcome. Listen to them, [and] know your own gaps. I try to make others feel they can challenge and come to me. I often don't know the answer, so I'll ask them questions. Focus on the process, not the outcome, and then the results will come.

AI: Leaders need to be confident in team members' responsibility to get the stuff done and deliver the outcomes. Moving away from monitoring inputs [is a] big shift for managers and HR. Time spent working is not a proxy for the quality of work being done.

CU: [With the rise in remote working], what has come down is the amount of time that leadership and team members spend with each other. Leaders now focus more on strategic issues and less on conversations with followers. Leaders must remember to ask the question, 'What impact am I having on others?'

Adult to Adult Interactions

Why is it so hard to have adult to adult conversations? We are derailed by rage, emotion, entitlement; we have been wronged, you don't like me, you think you are better than me … etc. Eric Berne was a psychiatrist who defined a model describing interactions between people; he called it transactional analysis.[98] He noted that we each have three ego states, 'parent', 'adult' or 'child', which characterise how we think, speak and act during any moment of interaction. In the adult ego state, the person is more centred, better able to evaluate pros and cons, more likely to enquire and gather data or ask clarifying questions, to reason logically and is more willing to take responsibility.

The healthiest interactions occur from adult to adult. However, to enter into such a state and remain there during the entire interaction is very hard as we tend to quickly move to one of the other ego states, thereby establishing less effective interactions. 'Parent' – 'child' transactions are very common between leaders (acting like the parent) and followers (acting like the child). If the goal of the leader is to have the most productive interactions possible with those around them, they must make the deliberate choice to step away from the ego state of 'parent' and to help raise the other person from 'child' so that then they can both interact adult to adult. Achieving and maintaining such shifts in ego states requires that both parties, particularly the leader, respect each other, their thoughts, and opinions. I characterise this as the willingness to see each other as an ally. There may be significant role and hierarchical differences between the two people but seeing each other as allies can facilitate a dramatic shift in the effectiveness of the interactions and resultant behaviours.

Balance Advocacy and Inquiry

The technique of productive reasoning[99] leads to greater mutual understanding and results in mutual commitment to a pathway forward. The concept and techniques of Productive Reasoning were pioneered by Chris Argyris and Donald Schon and first published in 1974. Chris Argyris was Professor Emeritus at Harvard

Business School. He noted that *'Smart people don't learn ... because they have too much invested in proving they know and avoiding being seen as not knowing'*. As a result of this predisposition not to learn from one another, Argyris described how conflict often emerges between individuals because they argue with each other from the top of their respective 'ladders of inference'.[100] A 'ladder of inference' (Figure 13.1) is when, through our personal experience and education, we have climbed up from the available data to recognise patterns that help us assess the situation. Then, we move farther on up the 'ladder' to choose actions that might be appropriate, as they have proven to be effective in the past.[101] In short, we argue from positions that reflect our respective experiences and assumptions but might be unanchored in the current data. The 'rungs' in the ladder of inference are (1) our selection from all the available data/facts, (2) our interpretation of the selected data, (3) assumptions that we make about the situation as we see it, (4) the conclusion that we draw, typically based on previous experience, (5) our personal beliefs as to what desired outcomes would be for the situation, and (6) our choice of actions to achieve our desired outcomes.

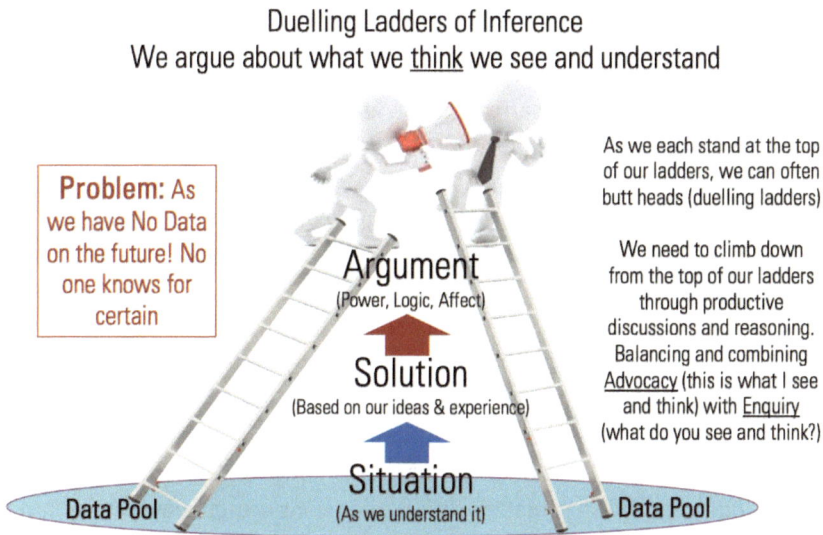

Source: Chris Argyris. The executive mind and double-loop learning. *Organizational Dynamics,* Autumn 1982.

Figure 13.1

IS: [For a] high quality of dialogue, get issues on the table, [and] make yourself vulnerable. Senior management must deal with complex problems – if they are not complex, then someone more junior should address them. [Aim for] Argyris's balance of advocacy and inquiry. Focus on the performance of the team – with the right behaviours. Make sure you are having data/evidence-based discussions rather than emotion, speculation, and rumour.

WS: I create an open culture whereby the decision-making can be challenged, and proper debate happens. From time to time, you will change your mind in response to what others have brought. I don't like the word diversity as it is overused. But I need to create a space where people with different views can disagree and contribute.

RB: The ability to run a great meeting for more than five people is rare. It's like [being] the conductor of an orchestra.

Argyris and Schon coined the expression 'double-loop learning'. The first 'loop' is to apply established decision-making rules and processes to achieve the desired goals. However, when the outcomes are not as intended, or an agreement cannot be reached a second 'loop' is undertaken. This is to explore the assumptions of each other and those embedded in how the problem has been defined. This second loop is intended for mutual learning; it can lead to creativity and innovation and reframe what seem to be paradoxical situations. Double-loop learning can also resolve tensions between colleagues, providing a common language and approach to explore differences and work together to find better solutions. In practice, it is important to balance enquiry with advocacy, i.e., to seek to equally weigh the time spent asking questions that explore the other person's logic, thinking and insight and the time spent explaining your own insight and thinking.

Reinforce Your Credibility

Credibility is perishable and doesn't come automatically with position! You are making judgement calls and making difficult decisions without data on the future. Most decisions must be revisited as the operations and marketplace develop and more insight and data become available. Your credibility can be eroded in the eyes of followers who have not been a part of or witnessed the decision-making process or do not feel that they were listened to or are otherwise not invested in the decisions. Credibility is crucial for leadership; it always has been – but is more so now. Why? Because you are much more exposed, more decisions have to be taken in uncertainty; there is greater visibility of those decisions and what transpired. Also, there is less trust in authority (position). Now more than ever, leaders must invest continuously in building and guarding their credibility.

WS: The two things that I look to create in my staff are (1) that they respect me, I have done the jobs that I ask them to do, that I walk the talk, I lead from the front, that I am capable in this role and (2) that they trust me to be making the right decisions – on balance, not all the time of course; we all make errors.

JV: The essence of a good decision is not just what comes out of it – the results (which you might not know for years), but fundamentally whether people understand it; can you explain it, and do they believe in the process by which this decision was reached? Credibility. You must build credibility, and you build it upwards. You build by achieving or exceeding your plan – a declared plan that everyone's expectations have been built around. Credibility upstream is important to be given the resources you need to achieve the plan.

AB: Leaders have always been leaders of people, but the factors that define you as a credible leader have changed completely. Until recently, your seniority, ultimately your power, was a sufficient condition to be respected and followed as a leader. Now, no more. You must gain credibility every day on the field in front of continuously evolving expectations regarding the environment, human rights, business practices, management style, personal behaviour, compensation standards, health and safety precautions, and many more. You have to prove your credibility every day.

The *Oxford Dictionary* definition of 'credibility' is the quality that somebody/ something has that makes people believe or trust them. So, credibility is closely associated with trust. Are you trusted to make the right decisions for the enterprise? Are you trusted to look after the employees? Credibility is not the same as trust, however, as credibility can be developed more quickly than trust. 'She's really credible; she led our competitor through a similar transformation before joining us'. In the book *Influence: The Psychology of Persuasion*,[102] Robert Cialdini highlights three techniques that can be particularly helpful in establishing credibility.

- **Commitment and consistency:** Being seen to be committed to a task or cause that resonates with others enhances their bias to believe that you have good reasons for your decisions. Even more so, when you are known to decide (or act) and display high commitment consistently. Consistency must also be observed between what you say and what you do (walking the talk). In today's world, that consistency needs to extend through all aspects of your life – what people see you are doing and saying in your private life, as highlighted through social media (yours or others), will impact your credibility in the workplace as a leader. The need for consistency is highly evident for political leaders and increasingly is demanded of all leaders.

- **Social proof:** Being seen as part of a group with credibility in a given domain reinforces your credibility. Are you a member of the professional association, are you invited to speak at the association, and have you been quoted on the blog/website of the association? Your credibility is enhanced by association with others who are credible. This can, however, be manipulated, as a financial donation to an association or forum may result in an invitation to join the executive committee or similar.

- **Authority:** A 'stamp of approval' or certificate may enhance your perceived credibility. You may have graduated from a particular course or school or held a notable position in a highly respected, well-known corporation. However, once in post in a new-to-you organisation, you must build and reinforce your credibility each day.

Credibility inside the enterprise, rather than external endorsement, significantly impacts your ability to lead. This requires being active and visible in sharing insights and opinions in meetings, forums and media. It also means being recognised for being associated with identifiable achievements. *What can you point to as your achievements in your current role?*

Pause, Reflect and Experiment: Bring Others With You

(1)   What is the 'shadow' you cast?
  - Are you demonstrating Adult-to-Adult interactions?
  - Are you practising Productive Reasoning, balancing your own advocacy with equal enquiry of the opinions of others (especially if they disagree with you)?
  - Is there a strong sense of trust and Psychological Safety? What else can you do to increase it?

(2)   Is the culture of your enterprise more towards "Ask Permission" or more towards "Ask Forgiveness"? Are people expected, empowered and rewarded for taking the initiative or executing on tasks they have been assigned?
- Where can you delegate or empower more?
- How do you respond when those you have delegated to or empowered struggle?
- Do you coach and equip people to grow and succeed, or is the culture more of catching errors and providing critical feedback?

(3)   What initiatives can you seed or scale in order to make the culture more constructive, more productive for others
- What can you change in your behaviours/interactions?
- How can you expand awareness and the increase the skills required for more productive interactions throughout the enterprise?

Chapter 14
Learn Faster

Time and energy are limited: Learn faster.

Around 1900, the rate at which human knowledge would double was approximately 100 years. By 1945, it would take only 25 years to double. Now, estimates are between 13 months and 12 hours, depending on who you listen to! What this means is that we must all adopt the behaviours and mindset of continuous learning. This is especially true for leaders, as they need to look over the horizon to see what's next and make decisions that integrate insights and opinions from an increasing array of experts. A few years ago, I was involved in designing a new degree programme to be launched by the university I was attached to. It took approximately six months to design the curriculum the best part of two years to pass through all the internal approvals and alignment meetings. They could then start advertising and recruiting for the first intake the following year. By the time the first cohort of students graduated from the programme, approximately half of what they had learned was no longer cutting-edge; almost seven years had passed since starting on the design. Graduating from a course cannot be seen as the end of learning; rather, it must be seen as the beginning of continuous, in-career, learning—a continual race to keep up with the knowledge being created. Effort is required to be continually learning. A mindset shift is required to accelerate your development.

We all learn and develop in response to stimuli, so it is critical to find the combination of stimuli that works best for you – and build learning and self-development into your daily, weekly, or monthly regime. In this chapter, I do not compare the merits of different stimuli; instead, I reflect on the array cited by the panellists. As you reflect on the comments below, I encourage you to note specific ideas to add to your self-development routine.

BJ: Jeff Immelt said he was selected to be CEO as 'people thought I could learn faster than others'. You have to ask yourself – am I learning faster than others – am I in a job, in a role, where I am learning faster than my peers? In this way, you create market value for yourself. If you don't want to learn new stuff, you should retire! Don't yell for help – buckle down and learn.

A key message from the panellists is the encouragement not to lose time. Put yourself in the best place possible to accelerate your impact or your development as a leader. If you are already an accomplished leader achieving the impact you want, then actively seek avenues to multiply your impact through influencing more broadly, or take on the challenges in an additional field. There is a shortage of competent leaders and there are big issues for society to address; don't slow down. Encourage and support others to also learn faster.

CM: There are growth industries that you want to think about aligning with. Think where that industry and your specialisations will be in 10 years – how relevant/in demand will your skills/experience be? Things are changing fast, so you don't want to become obsolete. Get tech industry exposure if you don't have it yet, as tech will be everywhere.

RB: Leadership is not evenly distributed in the world. There are many environments that do not require great leaders; they just need managers and executives. Therefore, put yourself into environments with lots of dislocation; at least, there is the possibility for leadership to emerge. Only there will there be the need to shape things rather than only optimise things.

SG: Think hard about how you are using your time and life. Make conscious choices about who you work for and with and what you are doing with your passion. Will you bring that to bear inside your organisation, or just think you'll watch the clock and check in and out? Where will you spend your emotional energy?

KC: Make hard choices early in your career and stick with them. There is a lot of opportunity to experiment in your career – but most will not work out. Take the decision: 'How important is money, status, and power to you?' You need to work this out for yourself. Then, decide how you want to fit in the system of the world, and then make your choices aligned with this. Do not get trapped in the middle – not pursuing your dreams, not racing to the top of an organisation or not building an enterprise for yourself. So many lives are wasted through compromise, working to make money to live but not living. Have a great coffee shop in a town you love and enjoy your life, or be an activist or a poet – do something that you really care about – that doesn't pay you – OR, if you want money and power, then be aggressive about it – do not settle for the slow career path and the hope of better things and promotions to come.

Change Tracks and Stretch Assignments

Staying in one career track will help you develop depth and specialist knowledge, but your rate of learning will be faster by exploring different tracks. Not everything you learn or experience will be immediately relevant to your next steps, but your breadth of experiences and insights will make you a stronger and better leader wherever you do go. I'm not suggesting that you change track every few months but do seek experiences that broaden your perspective and accelerate your learning and development. Individuals who stay within one track often struggle to understand their own capabilities as a leader, they may simply have survived a political process within one organisation or sector.

PC: At some stage, start a business – be entrepreneurial – this will show you how you lead ... do it as a side hustle or as your main thing – either way – do it and test yourself, grow and know yourself through this.

RP: I never said 'no' to a promotion opportunity I was offered, inside or outside the company I was working for. I often did not feel ready to take on the new role, but obviously, the person offering me the role saw something in me that gave them confidence to make me the offer. The moves were often extremely challenging; they stretched me and reshaped me. Then, soon enough, another opportunity would come along to be stretched again. My advice is never to say no to a step-up opportunity.

CM: [I had a] diversity of experience in big companies, start-ups, different industries, different countries – this allowed me to understand more quickly what was going on – and see what was going on faster than others – as I'm not so blinkered. It's empowered me to hire more broadly and try out new things in the market – rather than sticking with deep industry-experienced people or trying only what's been done before. [In] a start-up – [you need to be] scrappy, be agile in your thinking, and be hungry – this helps in the corporation now. I go faster as a team than others would expect. Corporate experience is necessary for governance – there is real value in understanding how others/departments, etc. – would be impacted. It's really helpful having had both ways of thinking – and then seeing how to combine the best parts of both models: a balance of diversity of experience. Having had both successes and failures is really important. You have to have humility – to understand the importance of learning and asking others for feedback. My quarterly team meetings cover what we have succeeded with and failed on – and what we have learned from both. We share these stories. It's really important to know where you have failed, be honest about it, and then own it and have the confidence to investigate and understand why you failed. Starting a career in consulting is super helpful. [It involves] structured thinking, numeracy, being challenged, working under pressure, and working in teams: foundational things [that are] so very, very important. Some time spent in sales is also critical – learning how to create, identify and jump on opportunities. How do I sell, orchestrate, and close on opportunities? Time in sales [teaches you] how to change the situation to create the opportunity.

KC: Find an impossibly difficult situation – a crazy goal requiring paradoxical thinking. Anyone can lead in an easy situation. Set an audacious goal and go for it; figure it out.

Live and Work Internationally

JH: Living in different countries and learning different cultures [helps]. I'm French; my experiences in Taiwan, China, the UK, Australia, the US, the Philippines and Singapore have all taught me a lot about how many different ways you can interpret, analyse or understand the world and people's behaviour and values. There is so much richness in a diversity of points of view, and this is something I will again embrace in my new role.

SB: My Asia experience was a huge benefit – I was well versed in things that others only encountered in the crisis – e.g., managing virtual teams and caring for team members, not to mention the diversity of beliefs, cultures, languages and regulatory environments.

TS: International living: I understand so much about myself through the experiences of being international. Living anywhere and feeling at home there, [I am] a citizen of the planet – and [am] OK with that.

Assemble Support

Coaches and Mentors

SGJ: I had a coach who gave me space to develop. I wasn't being coached in the way I expected (I expected coaching to be very hands-on and directive). So, she coached me for a while in the way that I was expecting – it was a disaster – so then I understood that she understood in detail the best way to accelerate and develop each individual in the way that they needed. Everyone is different and needs development in different ways. A great coach understands you and how to support your development to be the best that you can be. Focus on the person – and then the performance will come. This is now the foundation of my whole leadership philosophy.

SG: Mentors are so important. [xxxx] was and is mine, and I can't believe how lucky I was and continue to be to have her advice. She just helped a number of you, young, naive, hopeful people like me, which is where I was on the first step of the ladder, trying to get the courage and confidence to believe that I could make a bit of a change in the organisation, no matter how small. It was really critical she was proactive, poked me, introduced me to people, recommended books for me to read, and got me into doing lectures and stuff that I wouldn't have done. When I went to her with a particular business challenge I was working on, all of this was unofficial and completely free. [It's about] taking a step back and having a discussion as you would with business friends; she will just ask questions and prod me to be braver, and I think that was the thing; working in big corporations, one is in normally so constrained by all of the norms and hierarchy and fear of treading on someone's toes or looking like you are stepping out of your lane.

MH2: Reverse mentoring is also powerful because one of the huge problems in leadership is that you carry into the C-Suite all the values, behaviours and beliefs you acquired along your way – and you're stale. You get staler because status isolates you.

Colleagues and Peers

MH2: It's also really useful meeting with other senior leaders. I don't know any leader who has gone through a crisis (and they'll go through one at some point or another) without friends who are business leaders and understand what it's like. People standing on the edges can't even begin to understand, so having friends in your shoes in a different business is a really important safety valve. I would never appoint anybody that didn't have that support network.

SB: Having the mirror held up by the trusted people around you – you ask for it – and you need to trust them to do it with good intent. Ask for feedback – and then do something with the feedback!

Feed and Direct Your Curiosity

Curiosity is critical for the development of a leader. You must have curiosity about the world around you, the situation you are in and the people. Curiosity is having a strong desire to know or learn something. Directed curiosity is when curiosity is focused on a particular topic area, for example, relating to a new technology or area of challenge such as digital transformation.

DH: It's important to be curious about the future – not just reliant on the past. [It needs to be] curiosity directed by drive, not wide-eyed curiosity about 'everything': The drive to succeed [is] enabled by curiosity.

RB: Curiosity is fine – but it can be distracting, [as there are] too many rabbit holes – it needs to be in the service of the mission of the enterprise.

MH: Curiosity, directed curiosity, is in the service of your purpose and personal accountability – it leads to investigating and coming up with breakthroughs on the what, why, and how of the question, how do I shape markets and society in a different way? If you think you know it all – that is how you get lost.

CS: Being curious [is] not just about the external world's reality, but also one's inner thinking structures, which will be the most critical aspect of leadership for a better future.

PC: We need to open our minds more, listen more, with humility and understand where our own biases are. Be curious – you never stop learning.

It is important to stress that we are seeing the erosion, arguably the end of the notion that there are 'career paths' that should be followed. The concept of 'career path' can be traced back to the apprenticeship model, where a junior would learn at the foot of the master until eventually being deemed ready to take over the activity or business themselves or, indeed, to go out and create a similar business. For much of the past 70 years, this concept of progression has been built into the thinking of Human Resources practitioners. The HR officers and line managers decide the pace and progression steps the employee could make, whilst they retained control. In today's context, with the rebalancing of the relationship between follower and leader (or employee and executive) the pathways through which an individual develops are of little relevance. What matters are their skills and attitudes, the impact they can create, not how they came by them nor how long they have been in the workforce. As such, you should feel empowered to make your path one that fits how you best learn, and that will amplify the impact that you want to create.

PC2: There will be no dominant model of leadership – there is an endless variety of ways to lead – think of best fit, not best practice. We need all types of role models, an inclusive culture, different leadership styles, and different contexts. [This still needs to be] driven by principles: integrity, adaptability, agility, transparency, listening, etc. The best way to predict the future is to help to create it. This is perhaps the greatest responsibility of leaders today – to create a better tomorrow – to pioneer the new rather than perpetuate what is.

MH: Leadership will be divorced from the career path. Until now, career executives [have] eventually [been] in positions of leadership – they have survived the political processes of their organisations and demonstrated consistency as well as 'fit' with the cultural norms ... that's why they are ill-equipped to be leaders: leaders who actually make a difference.

Listen More

Listen carefully to other people's experiences, insights and observations on leadership, about you or the situations that you are facing. No one knows the whole truth; everyone has blind spots and biases, even you! It is important to remain open to hear and listen attentively to others' thoughts and opinions whilst also thinking critically for yourself.

WS: Listen to customers and get feedback: critical listening. They may have some insights that you must heed. They may be noisemaking. Also, listen to staff – we do leave interviews. Usually, people don't leave just for money. Reading these scripts can be very difficult – but highly valuable – again, you look for patterns, not just a single input.

CE: Listening skills – and having the opportunities to listen – create these opportunities and develop the skills. Build them into your plans – be professionally curious. Look beyond the world you are sitting in, e.g., economics or FT corporate networks and forums – have relationships outside of professional needs but opportunities to broaden minds and networks.

MG: Awareness of who you are leading. Focus on the people that you are leading. Seek to understand others.

MH: Although rare, it's phenomenally important to have opportunities to talk to people in your organisation at every level. Most leaders don't do it; they sit in their executive suite. Many are very afraid of their workforce – they need to get out more and listen much more. I think that will keep them in touch with what's happening in the world and break down many of their stereotypes and biases. I'm a very big fan of organisations that run shadow boards. They are designed to be a generation or two younger than the leadership team and demographically to look like the society or the market the company serves. I think it's phenomenal executive training for the younger people on those boards, and I think it's a fabulous way for leaders to learn details.

Pause, Reflect and Experiment: Learn Faster

(1) Make a plan of action for your development.
- Break the journey into milestones, steps, and timeframes.
- What are the daily disciplines you need to adopt? What to Start, Stop, Increase, Reduce? What accelerants can you build into your daily routine? (Reading, Listening)
- Decide that you will have a learning, 'growth' mindset. What experiences will you seek out, stepping beyond your comfort zone, beyond what you know, deliberately exposing yourself to learning and development challenges and opportunities in pursuit of your evolution?
- What development programmes or experiences will you participate in?

(2) Listen More: Practice Active Listening to fully sense what the other person is communicating.

(3) Who is in your support team, those you can confide in, who will provide you with honest, complete, and constructive feedback?
- What support can you assemble? (Coaches, Mentors, Internal and External Peers)
- Share your goal and plan with a confidante and ask them to hold you to account. Share with them your progress log at key milestone dates.
- Require that they give positive reinforcement and hold you accountable for the progress you have or have not made.

(4) Be transparent and accountable for your progress.
- How will you measure your progress on each aspect of your self-development journey?
- Keep a log of your progress and when and how you overcame or succumbed to derailing behaviours.
- What are your fears as you envisage the journey ahead of you, and how will you overcome them?

(5) Build resilience into your development of the plan. Your journey will not be smooth; you will make mistakes, and there will be times when you wantonly will not do what you have committed to yourself to do.
- How will you avoid becoming victim to 'all or nothing' thinking? Prepare now what will be your thought process and action plan to get yourself back on track when derailing situations occur.

PART SIX
Summary and Parting Advice

Chapter 15
Summary: Antidote to the Crisis of Leadership

Collective intent follows individual action.

There is a crisis of leadership as the demands and expectations placed on leaders have changed but most people in leadership positions are struggling to evolve their skills, practices, and mindsets to match this new reality. Most enterprises report a shortage of leaders today and insufficient in development for the future. The number and scale of scandals due to failures of leadership in enterprises, government and non-profits continue to escalate rapidly. Significant superior value is created by enterprises that are orientated to lean into the uncertainty and systemic complexity of the unfolding future. The outcomes of leadership not fit for the demands of today are unsustainable; reflected in the declaration by the United Nations of the requirements for development to be sustained and the World Health Organisation's identification of the epidemic of stress as one of the most serious threats to the global population and economic growth. Many people currently in leadership positions have been caught 'wrong-footed' by the changes in the demands and context of leading; they have learned how to lead through accumulating experience, observing role models, and participating in development programmes that were anchored in a now obsolete reality.*

DH: Now we need real leaders, not executives in leadership positions [...] There are changes in business due to technology (efficiency) and changes due to shifts in the macro environment. The biggest impact on global businesses comes from the macro geopolitical, etc., changes – so these are the most important issues for a CEO to navigate, where leaders create the most value – it's not through improving operations in a relatively stable environment! For 30 years, we wanted to be global – now we don't – that's a massive change to navigate. We need leaders who can get us through this now – not ask questions of others – just get on with it.

SG: Before the pandemic, a CEO was pretty much expected to run the business and be judged by the results and numbers, a fairly simple definition of what

---

* An example of this is the episode of the 'kiss', and reaction to the 'kiss', by the Spanish Football Association President to the winners of the Women's World Cup 2023.

success looks like. Now, suddenly, the environment in which they're operating is so much more complex. In VUCA, nobody knows what's going on. Still, they have to respond very quickly and do many different things beyond what they have been taught in business schools – social stuff, economic stuff, political stuff, and environmental stuff.

CS: Today's complexities and uncertainties are frightening many 'leaders'. Good leaders must develop the ability and capacity to understand the complexity that is inherent in today's world and develop other leaders to do the same.

RS: Focusing on internal issues and results is no longer good enough. In the past, leaders could immerse themselves in their industry, firm, and people. The leader of the future must be adept in understanding global issues, political, social, environmental, technological, economic, legal, etc., not only to understand but also develop positions for the firm and navigate the complexity of these factors on a global scale. Perhaps leaders must not only have an MBA but also some training in sociology, political economics, and global risk management.

The antidote to the crisis of leadership is the accelerated adoption of the skills and mindsets required for success today and tomorrow, by a broad population of existing and emergent leaders. More people with the right skills achieving positive outcomes. Achieving such a movement requires ensuring that many more people are (1) aware of the changes in the context of leadership, (2) recognise their need, and have the desire to evolve their prowess as a leader, (3) know what skills and mindsets to adopt (or amplify) and (4) are deliberate in driving their development. The antidote is more people embracing the four 'A's described in this book.

• **Aspire:** Stand firm on the Purpose, Values and Stakeholder Interests that you choose to represent. 'Aspire' is about having personal goals and values, while 'inspire' is about motivating and influencing others through actions, words, or achievements. If you don't aspire, how will you inspire others? If your only motivation is to generate your own wealth, then it may be hard to motivate others to join or stay with you in your quest! If you mouth the words of meaningful mission and positive future, but your own actions run contrary, you will lose moral authority, mistrust will grow, and followership will diminish, which may spiral into scandal as you come under increasing pressure and scrutiny. Yet you cannot please everyone all the time on everything! You must decide who and what you represent. It requires courage to stand for and be accountable for the choices you make, especially when faced with intense criticism. You must know the values that you will stand firm on, that will always and consistently guide your decision making, that you are comfortable and confident to be known for and held accountable to.

- **Ally:** Connect and collaborate broadly whilst helping others to thrive. Alliances involve cooperative collaboration between independent entities for mutual benefit, while a hierarchy denotes an authority-based structure where one entity holds a position of higher power or control over another. As a leader today, you must adopt the mindset of 'alliance', as stakeholders (employees, customers, investors, communities, media, etc.) are mobile, they move towards leaders they think align with their interests and needs and away from others. You are a leader because you have followers; you need followership from direct and indirect stakeholders. Recognise that relationships will change, possibly significantly, over time: A staff member today may be a vocal social-media critic tomorrow, a competitor today may be an investor in your company tomorrow. The leader with an alliance mindset understands that each person critically assesses if the ongoing (or intended) collaboration is valuable to them. Increasing followership requires the consideration of multiple factors, including promoting well-being and personal growth, the development of future relevant skills, providing meaning and purpose, the freedom to adhere to their personal values and attend to their economic needs. Leader-follower relationships are personal, social-media disintermediates and fuels the expectation for direct communications; today's leaders cannot be remote.

- **Adapt:** Increase the Dynamic Capacity of the enterprise and the mobility of resources. 'Adaptable' emphasises the capacity to adjust and change as needed, even if the adjustments are substantial, while 'agile' places more emphasis on speed, flexibility, and the ability to navigate change through iterative processes. The two can often complement each other in dynamic and ever-changing environments. Leaders today must be able to navigate in turbulence. Uncertainty is expected and systemic interactions ensure all situations are complex. A leader today can't make plans hoping for stability nor rely on stakeholder tolerance and rushed agility when surprised by reality. Include stakeholders in recognising and responding to the dilemmas, not shielding them from the complexity and jeopardy. Build up and leverage the Dynamic Capabilities of the enterprise (1) to Sense and Make Sense, (2) to Seize and Replicate, (3) to Reconfigure and Reposition. Increase the mobility of resources (talent, financial, knowledge, physical). Continuously strive to increase productivity through smarter working, expanded application of technologies and reduction of operational complexity. Adaptive leaders demonstrate humility, courage, and attentiveness to emergent indicators, they are not blinkered by past decisions nor overly adherent to current structures, they recognise and challenge legacy assumptions and practices.

• **Accelerate:** Time is short, and your energies are finite; learn faster. 'Accelerate' emphasises increasing the pace of progress, while 'continuous' communicates the need for on-going, consistent development; both are important mindsets for leaders today. Whether you are an emergent or highly experienced leader you need to learn more and learn faster. The shallowness of the existing leadership bench and the weakness of the pipeline of leaders in development are concerns of approximately three-quarters of businesses. The crisis is, in part, created by the rate of obsolescence of traditional approaches to leadership as the breadth of issues, the speed of change and the rate of knowledge creation accelerate. Awareness of the need and opportunity to accelerate personal development must be increased through constructive engagement and support; what was good previously must be built on and adjusted to match the context of today. Put yourself into the roles, sectors, markets, and challenges that will most accelerate your learning and development. Build supportive relationships with others who are facing similar issues and opportunities. Expand your knowledge through connecting broadly. Role model learning and support others to accelerate their development.

We don't know the future, but we can shape it. Or, more correctly, we are shaping it by what we do and by what we don't do, by what we stand for and by what we choose not to call out, challenge or change. The antidote to this crisis is for many more individuals to step forward, to build and apply the skills and mindsets required for success today. The greater the turbulence and rate of change in the contexts in which we live, the greater the opportunity to shape the future, if we have capable leaders.

I hope that you have found insights in this book useful for your own reflection and that you are motivated to further strengthen your prowess as a leader. I also hope you will encourage others to accelerate their development, and that they in turn will inspire others. Together, let's build momentum. Together we are the antidote to the crisis of leadership.

Chapter 16
Encouragement from the Panellists

Do the bit you can, the impact will spread and grow.

Mentors are a source of great support in a leader's journey, as highlighted in the chapter 'Accelerate'. As such, I asked each of the panellists for a few words of advice to share with you. As with the network of mentors that you establish, you will quickly note that the comments of any mentor reflect the life lessons and leadership journey of the individual giving the advice. Some common themes exist, but no two pieces of advice are identical; this is also one of the key reasons why you should engage with more than one mentor. This selection is not meant to be a substitute for you creating your own community of mentors. It is a collection of well-intended and heartfelt insights that come from the experiences of the panellists.

SG: How do you want to be in 5–10 years? Or even after you're retired, when you're looking back on your working career, what do you want to have done? Then why don't you start on that today?

PL: Understand where the revenue comes from and do what it takes to strengthen this function. Have direct involvement with customers; you can only be an effective leader if, at some point, you have personally driven sales.

BH: You can change the world – don't be afraid to do it. Changing the world could be for ten people or 10 million – impact other's lives for the better. It's a ripple effect.

AK: You have to be having a great time – having fun. Running an organisation is a privilege, but if it is grinding you down – if you are not loving it – then find a different organisation or role.

TC: Be prepared for stuff that's not understood. Be prepared for aspects of work that can't be comprehended. Don't be frightened to face it. Seek to understand. Be brave to ensure that decisions are informed.

IS: A clearly articulated strategy rooted in customer needs with a clear economic model: communicate it well, working with a great team.

SB: Get involved and be visible outside your day job: be known for more than just the transactional role that you have and are being paid for.

JV: Luck is important. Make yourself available. Hard work is [also] important; 'the harder you work, the more luck you experience'. Work hard on the things that you can control.

SB2: As humans, we impact how people feel – as a leader, this needs to be front and centre of our thinking.

KH: Make people want to follow you – give them a reason … and give them reasons to want to keep following you.

EB: Live your life detaching work performance from identity. Once that happens, you can become a leader because you are becoming more and more selfless.

OL: Think about leadership carefully; weigh it. Take the time to reflect. Understand yourself. Place those you are leading and the collective endeavour before yourself. Consider the impact your personal shadow has on the organisation and externally. Understand your values, their relationship with your mission, and how you conduct yourself. Care deeply for other people. Remember that moral courage trumps all – but you have to use it.

DL: Know that different paths/decisions can get you to the result you want; don't choose between them on the basis of popularity – do things, maybe the longer way, but stay true to your values.

CU: The leaders of tomorrow are probably already leaders today; tomorrow, they may be leading organisations and enterprises, but today, they are leading themselves. You are preparing yourself for the person you need to be tomorrow. You are focusing your energies on shaping your skills, abilities and impact to be relevant tomorrow.

SM: Be a force for good. Be audacious – 'swing for the fences' (put every ounce into succeeding, just going for it). Be generous. Be infectious. Get in the boxing ring of life. Then, a new world will open up for you. Inspire more people to go on their journey. Live without the regrets of what you didn't do.

PM: 'Think to the finish'. This was said by Field Marshal Allenbury, known as 'The Bull', of the 5th Lancers in 1902. 'Think to the finish'. You may have to make that quick decision; if I do, what will the 2nd or 3rd order consequences be – and what do I do to offset those consequences? Act quickly while still thinking – don't act recklessly. Intuition is important, seat-of-pants stuff, but offset risk by 'thinking to the finish'. Business is an art, not a science. It is waged between human beings and leaders and involves the interplay of their respective characters. There are lots of actors whose actions can influence each other in many indirect and direct ways. You cannot model the entire system, as it is too complex. [...] Leadership is a uniquely human activity, and you must keep thinking to the finish.

RS: Good luck!

APPENDIX

Values Worksheet

Value	Rating (1-5)	Value	Rating (1-5)
Accountability		Commitment	
Accuracy		Communication	
Achievement		Community	
Adaptability		Compassion	
Affection		Competence	
Agreeableness		Complexity	
Amusement		Confidence	
Assertiveness		Connection	
Attentiveness		Conscientiousness	
Authenticity		Conservativeness	
Autonomy		Consideration	
Balance		Consistency	
Benevolence		Contemplation	
Boldness		Contribution	
Bravery		Control	
Brilliance		Conviction	
Calmness		Cooperation	
Candour		Courage	
Capability		Courteousness	
Career		Creativity	
Caring		Credibility	
Cautiousness		Curiosity	
Certainty		Decisiveness	
Challenge		Dependability	
Charisma		Determination	
Charity		Devotion	
Charm		Dignity	
Cheerfulness		Diligence	
Citizenship		Discipline	
Clarity		Discovery	
Comfort		Drive	

Value	Rating (1-5)	Value	Rating (1-5)
Dualism		Helpfulness	
Dutifulness		Honesty	
Efficiency		Honour	
Elegance		Hope	
Emotional control		Humanity	
Empathy		Humility	
Empowerment		Humour	
Encouragement		Independence	
Energy		Individualism	
Enthusiasm		Innovation	
Entrepreneurial		Insightfulness	
Equality		Inspiration	
Experience		Integrity	
Experience		Intensity	
Experimenting		Intimacy	
Fairness		Intuitiveness	
Faithfulness		Justice	
Family		Kindness	
Fidelity		Knowledge	
Fitness		Learning	
Flexibility		Liberty	
Foresight		Logic	
Forgiveness		Loyalty	
Freedom		Mastery	
Friendliness		Maturity	
Fun		Mindfulness	
Generosity		Moderation	
Gentleness		Neutrality	
Genuineness		Objectivity	
Graciousness		Open-mindedness	
Gratitude		Optimism	
Growth		Order	
Harmony		Organisation	

Value	Rating (1-5)	Value	Rating (1-5)
Originality		Selflessness	
Passion		Speed	
Patience		Spontaneity	
Performance		Stability	
Perseverance		Status	
Positivity		Structure	
Practicality		Teamwork	
Precision		Thoroughness	
Productivity		Tidiness	
Professionalism		Timeliness	
Punctuality		Tolerance	
Purpose		Tradition	
Recognition		Tranquillity	
Relatedness		Trust	
Reliability		Truthfulness	
Responsibility		Unity	
Restraint		Wellness	
Results-oriented		Willingness	
Rigour			

Endnotes

[1] Evans, L. 2021. 'Is Leadership a Myth? A "New Wave" Critical Leadership-Focused Research Agenda for Recontouring the Landscape of Educational Leadership.' *Educational Management Administration & Leadership* 50(3): 413–435.

[2] World Economic Forum, Future of Jobs Report, April 2023. https://www.weforum.org/reports/the-future-of-jobs-report-2023/

[3] https://sdgs.un.org/goals

[4] https://www.ddiworld.com/research/leadership-transitions-report.

[5] https://www.kornferry.com/insights/this-week-in-leadership/leadership-shortage-hr-survey

[6] Mackey, J., and R. Sisodia. 2014. *Conscious Capitalism*. Boston, MA: Harvard Business Review Publishing.

[7] https://hbr.org/2014/05/from-purpose-to-impact.

[8] https://hbr.org/2014/05/from-purpose-to-impact.

[9] Irving, J.A., and J. Berndt. 2017. 'Leader Purposefulness within Servant Leadership: Examining the Effect of Servant Leadership, Leader Follower-Focus, Leader Goal-Orientation, and Leader Purposefulness in a Large U.S. Healthcare Organization.' *Administrative Sciences*. MDPI, 7(2): 1–20.

[10] https://sdgs.un.org/goals.

[11] Mango, E. 2018. 'Beyond Leadership.' March. *Open Journal of Leadership* 7: 117–143. doi: 10.4236/ojl.2018.71007.

[12] Joseph, E., and B. Winston. 2005. 'A Correlation of Servant Leadership, Leader Trust, and Organizational Trust.' *Leadership & Organization Development Journal* 26(1): 6–22.

[13] Lowe, K., K. Kroeck, and N. Sivasubramaniam. 1996. 'Effectiveness Correlates of Transformational and Transactional Leadership: A Meta-Analytic Review of the MLQ Literature.' *The Leadership Quarterly* 7(3): 385–425.

[14] Avolio, B., and W. Gardner. 2005. 'Authentic Leadership Development: Getting to the Root of Positive Forms of Leadership.' *The Leadership Quarterly* 16(3): 315–338.

[15] Brown, M., and L. Treviño. 2006. 'Ethical Leadership: A Review and Future Directions.' *The Leadership Quarterly* 17(6): 595–616.

[16] Greenleaf, R. 1977. *Servant Leadership*. San Francisco, CA: Jossey-Bass.

[17] Burns, J.M. 1978. *Leadership*. New York: Harper and Row.

[18] George, B. 2003. *Authentic Leadership*. San Francisco, CA: Jossey-Bass.

[19] Cameron, K.S. and R.E. Quinn. 2005. *Diagnosing and Changing Organizational Culture: Based on the Competing Values Framework*. San Francisco, CA: John Wiley and Sons.

[20] George, William W. 2007. *True North: Discover Your Authentic Leadership*. San Francisco, CA: Jossey-Bass.

[21] Bennis, Warren G. 1989. *On Becoming a Leader*. Reading, MA: Addison-Wesley Pub. Co.

[22] Sinek, S. 2017. *Leaders Eat Last: Why Some Teams Pull Together, and Others Don't*. New York, NY: Portfolio/Penguin.

[23] http://timesofindia.indiatimes.com/home/opinion/interviews/If-leaders-fail-people-will-lead-Kofi-Annan/articleshow/29917567.cms.

[24] https://www.weforum.org/agenda/2019/12/davos-manifesto-2020-the-universal-purpose-of-a-company-in-the-fourth-industrial-revolution/.

[25] https://www.accenture.com/us-en/insights/consulting/responsible-leadership.

[26] Day, D.V. 2001. 'Leadership Development: A Review in Context.' *The Leadership Quarterly* 11: 581–613.

[27] Iles, P. and D. Preece. 2006. 'Developing Leaders or Developing Leadership? The Academy of Chief Executives' Programmes in the North East of England.' *Leadership* 2: 317–340.

28 Bolden, R. and J. Gosling. 2006. 'Leadership Competencies: Time to Change the Tune?' Leadership 2: 147–163.

29 De Rue, D.S., and S.J. Ashford. 2010. 'Who Will Lead and Who Will Follow? A Social Process of Leadership Identity Construction in Organisations.' *Academy of Management Review* 35: 627–647.

30 Krauss, S.E., J.A. Hamid, and I.A. Ismail. 2010. 'Exploring Trait and Task Self-Awareness in the Context of Leadership Development Among Undergraduate Students from Malaysia.' *Leadership* 6: 3–19.

31 Schyns, B., T. Kiefer, R. Kerschreiter, and A. Tymon. 'Teaching Implicit Leadership Theories to Develop Leaders and Leadership: How and Why It Can Make a Difference.' *Academy of Management Learning & Education* 10(3): 397–408.

32 Hansen, M.T., and Bolko von Oetinger. 2001, March. 'Introducing T-Shaped Managers: Knowledge Management's Next Generation.' HBR 79(3): 106–16.

33 https://www.mckinsey.com/featured-insights/diversity-and-inclusion/diversity-wins-how-inclusion-matters.

34 Dovidio, J.F., J.D. Johnson, S.L. Gaertner, A.R. Pearson, T. Saguy, and L. Ashburn-Nardo. 2010. 'Empathy and Intergroup Relations.' In *Pro-Social Motives, Emotions, and Behaviour,* edited by M. Mikulincer and P.R. Shaver. Washington, DC: American Psychological Association.

35 Kouzes, J.M., and B.Z. Posner. 2012. *The Leadership Challenge: How to Make Extraordinary Things Happen in Organisations* (5th ed.). San Francisco, CA: Jossey-Bass.

36 Kellett, J.B., R.H. Humphrey and R.G. Sleeth. 2002. 'Empathy and Complex Task Performance: Two Routes to Leadership.' *The Leadership Quarterly* 13(5): 523–544.

37 Goleman, D., R. Boyatzis, and A. McKee. 2002. *Primal Leadership: Realising the Power of Emotional Intelligence.* Boston: Harvard Press.

38 Family Friendly Working Hours Taskforce. 2010. Flexible working: working for families, working for business. Retrieved from http://www.cipd.co.uk/NR/rdonlyres/F36B815C-ABAF-4A04-8842-639EA20E48BD/0/Flexible_working_Taskforce_report.pdf.

39 Holt, S., and J. Marques. 2012. 'Empathy in Leadership: Appropriate or Misplaced? An Empirical Study on a Topic That is Asking for Attention.' *Journal of Business Ethics* 105: 95–105.

40 Anderson, H.J., J.E. Baur, J.A. Griffith, and M.R. Buckley. 'What Works for You May Not Work for (Gen) Me: Limitations of Present Leadership Theories for the New Generation.' *The Leadership Quarterly* 28(1): 245–260.

41 Goleman, D. 2000. 'Leadership That Gets Results.' *Harvard Business Review,* 78(2): 78–90.

42 Judge, T.A., and R.F. Piccolo. 2004. 'Transformational and transactional leadership: a meta-analytic test of their relative validity.' *J Appl Psychol.* 89(5): 755–768.

43 George, B. 2007. *True North: Discover Your Authentic Leadership.* Hoboken, NJ: Jossey-Bass.

44 Boyle, C.J., M. Gonyeau, S.K. Flowers, P. Hritcko, R. Taheri, and S. Prabhu. 2018. 'Adapting Leadership Styles to Reflect Generational Differences in the Academy.' *American Journal of Pharmaceutical Education* 82(6) Article 6886.

45 https://www2.deloitte.com/xe/en/insights/topics/value-of-diversity-and-inclusion/diversity-and-inclusion-in-tech/importance-of-allyship-women-in-tech.html

46 Walsh, B., S. Jamison, and C. Walsh. 2010. *The Score Takes Care of Itself: My Philosophy of Leadership.* Penguin Publishing Group.

47 Wyatt, S. 2020. *Management and leadership in the 4th Industrial Revolution.* New York, NY: Kogan Page.

48 Tuckman, B.W. 1965. Developmental sequence in small groups. *Psychological Bulletin,* 63(6): 384.

49 Hackman, R. 2002. *Leading Teams. Setting the stage for great performances.* Harvard Business School Press.

50 https://www.nytimes.com/2016/02/28/magazine/what-google-learned-from-its-quest-to-build-the-perfect-team.html

[51] Walsh et al., *The Score Takes Care of Itself.*
[52] https://hbr.org/2013/10/fergusons-formula.
[53] *Forbes online.* June 29th 2022. Dan Pontefract.
[54] https://www2.deloitte.com/us/en/insights/topics/leadership/employee-wellness-in-the-corporate-workplace.html.
[55] Wyatt, *Management and leadership in the 4th Industrial Revolution.*
[56] https://www.weforum.org/focus/fourth-industrial-revolution.
[57] World Health Organisation. https://www.who.int/occupational_health/topics/stressatwp/en/.
[58] https://www.un.org/esa/socdev/csocd/2019/Chancel2019CSD.pdf.
[59] https://joshbersin.com/2021/04/the-secret-to-wellbeing-at-work-is-leadership/.
[60] Wyatt, *Management and leadership in the 4th Industrial Revolution.*
[61] Pink, D. 2009. *Drive: The Surprising Truth About What Motivates Us.* Riverhead.
[62] https://neuroleadership.com/research/tools/nli-scarf-assessment/.
[63] https://www.myersbriggs.org/my-mbti-personality-type/mbti-basics/.
[64] https://hbr.org/2013/10/fergusons-formula.
[65] https://hbr.org/2021/02/company-culture-is-everyones-responsibility.
[66] Future of Jobs Report. 2023. World Economic Forum.
[67] CIPD. June 2019 June Flexible Working in the UK, page 2.
[68] Wrzesniewski, A. and J.E. Dutton. 2001. 'Crafting a Job: Revisioning Employees as Active Crafters of Their Work.' *The Academy of Management Review* 26.
[69] Rousseau, D.M., V.T. Ho, and Jerald Greenberg. 2006. 'I-Deals: Idiosyncratic Terms in Employment Relationships.' *Academy of Management Review* 31(4): 977–994.
[70] Bal, Matthijs, and D. Rousseau (eds). 2019. *Idiosyncratic Deals between Employees and Organisations. Conceptual issues, applications and the role of co-workers.* Routledge.
[71] Hammer, L.B., E.E. Kossek, N.L. Yragui, T.E. Bodner, and G.C. Hanson. 2009. 'Development and validation of a multidimensional measure of family supportive supervisor behaviors (FSSB).' *Journal of Management* 35(4): 837–856.
[72] https://www.forbes.com/sites/danpontefract/2022/06/29/leaders-are-living-in-well-being-la-la-land/
[73] Greenleaf, R.K. 1970. *The Servant as Leader.* Center for Applied Studies.
[74] https://www.greenleaf.org/what-is-servant-leadership/.
[75] Wyatt, *Management and leadership in the 4th Industrial Revolution.*
[76] Teece, D.J., G. Pisano, and A. Shuen. 1997. 'Dynamic Capabilities and Strategic Management.' *Strategic Management Journal* 18(7): 509–533
[77] Daniel, K. 2012. *Thinking Fast and Slow.* Penguin Random House.
[78] Mintzberg, H. 1994. 'The Fall and Rise of Strategic Planning.' *Harvard Business Review.* 72(1): 107–114.
[79] Hunt-Davis, B., and H. Beveridge. 2020. *Will it make the boat go faster? (2nd ed.).* Matador.
[80] https://en.wikipedia.org/wiki/Silvio_Scaglia.
[81] Leinwand, P., M.M. Mahadeva, and B. Sheppard. 2022, Jan/Feb. 'Reinventing Your Leadership Team.' *Harvard Business Review.* 100(1): 61–69.
[82] Research conducted by Prof. Steve Wyatt and Prof. Hitendra Patel, 2012.
[83] Leinwand, et al., 'Reinventing Your Leadership Team.'
[84] Rittel, H.W.J. and M. M. Webber. 1973, June. 'Dilemmas in a General Theory of Planning.' *Policy Sciences* 4(2).
[85] Heifetz, R., and D. Laurie. 2001. 'The Work of Leadership.' *Harvard Business Review* 79: 131–141.
[86] Tushman, M.L., and C. A. O'Reilly III. 2006. 'Ambidextrous organisations: Managing evolutionary and revolutionary change.' *California Management Review* 38(4): 8–29.

[87] Martin, R. 2007. *The Opposable Mind: How Successful Leaders Win Through Integrative Thinking.* Harvard Business School Press.

[88] Jurisic, N., M. Lurie, P. Risch and O. Salo. 2020 August. *Doing vs. being: Practical lessons on building an agile culture.* McKinsey & Co.

[89] https://hbr.org/2013/10/fergusons-formula.

[90] https://www.mcchrystalgroup.com/library/team-teams-new-rules-engagement-complex-world/.

[91] https://www.reinventingorganizations.com/.

[92] Solbrig, L., B. Whalley, D.J. Kavanagh, J. May, T. Parkin, R. Jones, and J. Andrade. 2019. ‚Functional imagery training versus motivational interviewing for weight loss: a randomised controlled trial of brief individual interventions for overweight and obesity.‘ *International Journal of Obesity,* 43(4): 883–894.

[93] https://www.selfleadership.com/.

[94] Maxwell, John C. 2008. *Make Today Count: The Secret of Your Success Is Determined by Your Daily Agenda.* United States, Center Street.

[95] https://youtu.be/d8Wn3-BhPqw.

[96] Maxwell, J.C. 1998. *The 21 Irrefutable Laws of Leadership.* Nashville: Thomas Nelson.

[97] Blanchard, K., and P. Hodges. 2003. *The Servant Leader: Transforming Your Heart, Head, Hands & Habits.* Nashville: Thomas Nelson.

[98] Berne, E., 1958. ‘Transactional analysis: A new and effective method of group therapy.’ *American Journal of Psychotherapy* 12(4), 735–743.

[99] Argyris, C., and D. Schon. 1974. *Theory in practice: Increasing professional effectiveness.* Jossey-Bass.

[100] Argyris, C., 1970. *Intervention Theory & Method: A Behavioral Science View.* Reading, MA: Addison-Wesley.

[101] Argyris, C., 1971. *Management and Organisational Development. The Path from XA to YB.* New York, NY: McGraw-Hill.

[102] Cialdini, R.B. 2007. *Influence: The Psychology of Persuasion.* Vol. 55. New York: Collins.

About the Author

Stephen (Steve) Wyatt, is an experienced business leader and consultant, who believes strongly in the importance of developing and empowering talent and leadership. He is currently also a professor of Leadership and Strategy at the University of Bath, UK. Professor Wyatt was formerly a Regional Managing Partner of Monitor Group (Monitor Deloitte) and a partner with Heidrick & Struggles Leadership Consultancy. He is the author of four books. The two most recent discuss leadership and management in the accelerated, digitally enabled context of the 4th Industrial Revolution. Through his consulting and teaching he shares his insights to enhance the effectiveness of leaders and the performance of enterprises. Now living in the UK, he has extensive international experience, having been based in Asia and Europe for almost 30 years.

Steve Wyatt brilliantly points out the evolving expectations of employees on modern leaders and how increasing scrutiny, transparency and judgement reshape the landscape of leadership. Reassuringly he also lays out the opportunities these changes present, offering pragmatic, sensible and actionable solutions for those courageous enough to experiment with their leadership approach.

Robert Palmer, Vice President, Carnival UK

A tried, tested and proven leader, Steve has grown enterprises in complex, multi-sector and multi-cultural environments: He is also a consummate consultant and teacher. His first-hand experience, structured thinking and research rigour are always evident.

Mark Hewett, Vice President, Energy & Utilities. Capgemini

I had the good fortune to work with Steve during an important time, accelerating my impact as a global female leader. His teaching style, mentorship and innovation models are world-class and continue to serve me well.

Tonika Sealy-Thompson, Ambassador of Barbados to Brazil

Steve Wyatt has lived the most extraordinary and adventurous life, taking on breath-taking business and societal challenges across different parts of the world. He has a remarkable capacity to notice new ways of looking at things and a deep passion to teach these ideas and notions to others. Full of insights about our changing world and the implications for every leader whilst providing tools and support for how to lead and be.

Simon (Mac) McKenzie, CEO, The Bridge Institute

Steve is one of the most inspirational and impactful leaders I have had the pleasure of working with. We have collaborated across various sectors and countries over the past 20 years, achieving extraordinary outcomes and positively impacting others. Steve distils his deep pool of experience into actionable messages. His sharp insights on thriving as a leader are particularly relevant in today's turbulent and complex context.

Patrick Corr, Entrepreneur and Business Leader, Indeed.com

Index